One Step More, Lord!

One Step More, Lord!

Opha Bingham
WITH
Robert E. Bingham

BROADMAN PRESS
Nashville, Tennessee

Unless otherwise noted, Scripture quotations are from the King James Version of the Bible. Quotations marked RSV are from the Revised Standard Version of the Bible, copyrighted 1946, 1952, © 1971, 1973. Quotations marked Moffatt are from *The Bible: a New Translation,* by James A. R. Moffatt. Copyright © 1935 by Harper and Row, Publishers, Inc. Used by permission. The quotation marked Weymouth is from *Weymouth's New Testament in Modern English,* by Richard Francis Weymouth, published by special arrangement with James Clarke and Company, Ltd., and reprinted by permission of Harper and Row, Publishers, Inc.

Dewey Decimal Classification: B
Subject Headings: BINGHAM, OPHA // MULTIPLE SCLEROSIS—BIOGRAPHY
Library of Congress Catalog Card Number: 84-4942
Printed in the United States of America

Library of Congress Cataloging in Publication Data

Bingham, Opha, 1925-
   One step more, Lord!

   1. Bingham, Opha, 1925-   2. Multiple sclerosis—
Patients—Georgia—Atlanta—Biography.   3. Christian
life—Baptist authors.   I. Bingham, Robert E.   II. Title.
RC377.B54   1984   155.9′16   84-4942
ISBN 0-8054-5432-2

Dedicated to
My Family
and
My Greater Family

Contents

Foreword

Among God's best gifts to his children is the gift of friendship, the fellowship of kindred minds. I considered Opha Bingham my friend before I met her. I knew her best through her husband, what he said about her, and what he was. Because I did not know them in earlier years, I am sensitive to them as a unit, what they have become together. It is not possible to know them without the overwhelming impression of two people whom God has made one, connected by mutual love for each other and for Christ, directed by a mutual obedience to the working of the Spirit in them.

Although my work brings me often into contact with Bob, it was not until the summer of 1975 that I met Opha in the flesh. I will never forget that first meeting. We were in Stockholm, and I had arrived with some personal difficulty at the huge building where the opening session of the Baptist World Congress was about to begin. As I stepped off the bus and entered the building I saw Bob and Opha. My instant thought was, *How did they manage to get here with that wheelchair, when I found it so complicated to get here on two strong legs?*

From that day to this, I have never again thought of Opha and Bob as having a handicap. The most obvious visible thing about them is that wheelchair; that is, until you know them. Then the most obvious, though invisible, thing is that they are whole, two beings who function as one, two wonderful children of God who know that Christ did come to bring them abundant life.

I am glad that Opha has worked through this book. I am glad that Bob worked with her on it. Their story needs to be told. Just before I sat down to write this word I had mentioned the manuscript to a young woman in a meeting. She immediately wanted to know the title of the book, for her aunt had just been diagnosed as having multiple sclerosis. She felt that the book would help her aunt deal with her new way of life.

But I think the book will be more than an encouragement to those who live with a long-term illness. I think its best use will be by people who are as healthy as I am, but who earnestly want to share life with another who is not well. The practical suggestions, the personal anxieties, and the total humanity of the Binghams give testimony to the faith they exhibit.

CAROLYN WEATHERFORD
Birmingham, Alabama

Preface

Everyone is handicapped in some way—not as the public views the word *handicapped* but defined as anything that prevents you from achieving your goals. Some with finely tuned bodies do not have keen minds or contagious spirits. Others have limited human resources with which to cope in society.

For thirty-five years we have ministered to hundreds of families. They have opened their inner closets to our caring concerns. We have shared in their joys and in their sorrows. When they need some helpful guidance, they bring out the skeletons and do not mind "telling it like it is."

Knowing many people so personally, I can say that Bob and I would not trade places with any of them. We would not trade our situation with anyone we know. After taking inventory of all we have for which to be thankful, we feel, of all people, most blessed!

Naturally, depression is always lurking around the corner. To deny its proximity is to encourage it to come inside and live with you. The temptation to feel sorry for yourself is a first cousin of depression. Emotional bankruptcy has been avoided in my case by periodically assessing my emotional assets and liabilities. "Keeping up with the Joneses" has usually been attributed to financial and life-style comparisons. Come to think of it, it can just as easily apply to emotional health. As I said above, we would not trade places with the "Joneses."

The fear of the unknown is often compensated by the reality of the present. Usually we tend to depreciate our condition when comparing it to perfection. Life is not perfect. For the billions of people in the world, life is average: sometimes high, sometimes low, usually average. When I compare my physical being, it grades low in muscular control, but it grades high in overall general health. Other high marks are realized in family life, friends, home, peace of mind, fulfillment of eternal values, and on and on. Reality has its compensations when given a fair shake. Contrary to temptations of a blue Monday, the dice are not loaded against you.

Introduction

Before you want to read about my reactions and response to long-term illness, you deserve professional verification. These come from the surgeons and physicians who have walked with me through the medical mazes. They have provided you with documentation directly from their official records to authenticate my medical pilgrimage.

Likewise, there are letters from my pastors who have walked spiritual paths with me attesting to my desire to cope with long-term illness in the Christian tradition.

It seemed preferable to give you this information in introduction form rather than in the text of the book. First, we probably need it up-front. Second, we do not want to clutter up the flow of the chapters with pathological details.

The book is not a biography per se, although it must include some biographical material to give you the broad picture. Rather, it is an encouragement to those who relate to long-term illness: patients, their families, and friends.

Medical History

While the medical records total more than two hundred pages, they have been condensed to several excerpted and paraphrased paragraphs which recap and highlight the last twenty-five years.

William W. Moore, Jr., M.D.   December 2, 1982
Neurological Surgery
Atlanta, Georgia

Dear Opha,

I am enclosing copies of your clinical notes going back some
twenty years feeling that most people would like to get as close to
the original and accurate material as possible.

I have always admired the way you have tolerated and accepted
this problem or more particularly, these many problems without
ever having exhibited the "Why me?" attitude.

                                        Sincerely,
                                        William W. Moore, Jr., M.D.

Excerpts from Records:
SUMMARY

This lady with known multiple sclerosis since 1960 character-
ized by a steadily progressive spastic quadriparesis, more severe on
the right side than the left. Developed trigeminal neuralgia in 1979
involving the left second and third divisions. Operation performed
3/17/79: radio frequency lesioning of left trigeminal nerve. She
had a nephrectomy in 1966. She fractured her left hip in 1976 and
her right hip in 1979 with a prosthetic replacement of each hip.

J. Frank Harris, M.D.   December 21, 1983
Internal Medicine
Atlanta, Georgia

Dear Opha:

I first saw you in 1961 with typical symptoms of muscular
malfunctions and symptomatic problems. As time went by, the
symptoms of an illness of the central nervous system became more
and more manifest. The MS diagnosis was nailed down later.

No one but the patient can understand or appreciate the extent
and disability of this illness. My admiration for your handling of
MS is great, indeed. Throughout all of your several illnesses, I have
never known you to appear depressed. Your usually sunny counte-

nance, your eternal optimism, and your obvious faith has been very apparent as I have observed you in my office, our church, and at numerous social functions.

I believe you have coped most effectively with long-term illness. I do not know of anyone who has dealt with this chronic illness any better than you. I think Bob may have helped you through the living of these days.

To the outside world, it may not appear that you have as much disability as I know you must experience. You truly have been an inspiration to me as well as to the countless persons who know you.

Sincerely,
J. Frank Harris, M.D.

Harry L. Broome, M.D.   November 18, 1982
Orthopedic Surgery
Atlanta, Georgia

To Whom It May Concern:

On May 14, 1976, I met Opha Bingham who had an impacted femoral neck fracture on the left side following a fall. She had a diagnosis of multiple sclerosis. Subsequently, she had prosthetic replacement of the left femoral head. She followed her physical therapy program to the absolute letter and in a beautiful manner.

On February 12, 1979, she had another fall and had a fracture of the right femoral neck, and this was treated with prosthetic replacement of the femoral head. Just to make matters worse, she had a difficult episode of trigeminal neuralgia and had progression of her multiple sclerosis. Rehabilitation following her second operation was certainly more difficult than the first procedure. Two months later she had cutaneous neuralgia in each thigh.

She continues to live to the fullest and to serve as a source of learning and inspiration for me in demonstrating remarkable capacity for "making do."

Sincerely,
Harry L. Broome, M.D.

William Ainslie, M.D.   September 30, 1982
General Surgery
Niagara Falls, Ontario

To Whom It May Concern:
  So many long-term MS patients tend to feel sorry for themselves
and soon after lash out at everyone. Mrs. Bingham has obviously
made peace with herself and her world. She realistically accepts life
as she finds it and makes the best of it for herself and all those
around her. This operation was critical bordering on lethal. With
such abdominal pain, she did not complain. Later, I realized that
her faith was sustaining her. Her sweet spirit shines through.
                                        William Ainslie, M.D.

                          Pastoral Testimony
Dotson M. Nelson, Jr., Th.D.   December 17, 1982
Mountain Brook Baptist Church
Birmingham, Alabama

  I have known Opha Bingham since she was a young bride in
Kansas City, Missouri: vivacious, active, and a fully complete
companion for her husband both professionally in their home and
professionally as he served with three churches and then with the
Home Mission Board of the Southern Baptist Convention.
  During eight years of this observation, Bob and Opha were
colaborers with me at First Baptist Church, Greenville, South
Carolina. I saw her become a fine and glorious mother to two
wonderful daughters and at the same time keep her mother-in-law
during her latter years. During this specific time, her multiple
sclerosis was coming on and she refused to be daunted. Always she
was the same innovative, creative, and interesting Opha Bingham.
  She had the wonderful art of taking what could be tragedy and
transforming it into triumph. She has had the experience of falling
. . . and laughing at herself, of making peace with a wheelchair, of
keeping going when it would have been easier to stop. She is a great
lady.

If I could point out one person to emulate with MS, Opha Bingham would be the first name on my list.

J. T. Ford, Pastor   December 11, 1982
Wieuca Road Baptist Church (1955-1963)
Atlanta, Georgia

Dear Opha:

Your splendid attitude and exemplary behavior in adjusting to multiple sclerosis has indeed been an inspiration to all who have known you during these twenty-two years.

I think these patterns of response are a witness of your sturdy character and your Christian faith. If sharing these insights through the printed page can encourage and inspire other pilgrims with similar problems, your pain and patience will have been somewhat rewarded.

Be assured of my continuing appreciation for your courage and your warm, noble spirit.

Sincerely,
J. T. Ford

SECTION ONE

Take Not to Thy Bed

1
Realizing the Truth

The physician uttered two of the most frightening words to vibrate through the human ear. "Mrs. Bingham, I am sorry to tell you that you have . . . MULTIPLE SCLEROSIS!"

After eighteen months of medical testing and retesting, hopes and fears, good dreams and bad dreams, it had all distilled down to two words: *multiple sclerosis.* (MS)! I had grown to fear those words during the diagnostic stages. I would grow to hate them as the disease developed.

What was going to happen to me? Our two young daughters? And my husband? Would I be a longtime drag on them? Would a long-term illness change my personality? Make me bedfast? Reduce opportunities for service? Wipe out the pleasures of life? Tempt me to become bitter? Perhaps most fearful, would it diminish my Christian faith? What would life hold in its mysterious hand?

During my teen and young adult years, living with long-term illness had not seriously entered my consciousness. Death was a reality, probably accidental. But I was not emotionally prepared for struggling day in, day out, year in, year out with a disease that would accompany me through my remaining years.

Would God miraculously intercede? I guessed he would if he wanted to. But would he want to? Faith healing was more than a tent meeting or television event. Surely, with my history of faith and good works, our countless Christian friends, and my desire to actively serve—he would bring complete healing to my body. Or would he?

Life to this point had been good—full of numerous blessings:

21

a devoted husband, two healthy daughters, living in our first new house. Bob was a minister at the historic First Baptist Church of Greenville, South Carolina. Church members and neighbors had been more than gracious to us. The days were filled with challenge. The years had been fulfilling in personal growth and achievement. I was intimately aware of God's blessings. What more could a young family want!

By now we had escaped many of the pitfalls that ensnare young couples coping in a secular society. It was 1959 and we were thirty-four years old. (I might as well begin this story by being honest about my age.)

"Energy" could have been my middle name. Perhaps every active homemaker feels that way. No day had enough hours to meet the demands. We had been married twelve years; our daughters were seven and five years old. Bob's income was enough to pay the bills and free me to be a full-time homemaker and participate in volunteer projects in the community and church.

I had been so involved in trying to help others that I scarcely had time for myself. (Surely, there was no time for any long-term illness!) Mother Bingham was in declining health, and it seemed best for her to move from Kansas City to live with us. No big deal. She was pleasant though continually incapacitated. Arteriosclerosis had shortened her memory and lengthened her need for hourly attention. While a drain on physical and emotional energy, it was a pleasure to make a loving home for her. Death was a typical package of mixed emotions—including relief for me.

While growing up on a farm in southwest Missouri, mother taught me to look for avenues of service to those in physical or emotional distress. Those seeds bore fruition as opportunities came to minister to those who were housebound, hospitalized, or bereaved. Bob often chided me about baking so many cakes, pies, and cookies for others, but our cookie jar was often empty.

Public school education meant so much to me. With our girls in school, now was my opportunity to show appreciation by assisting as a volunteer homeroom mother. The teacher made the suggestions and assignments. I made time to fill the needs. The PTA was another viable outlet of my gratitude. Fund-raising campaigns and paper sales used much of my abundant energy.

Being a minister's wife had its own demands (real and imagined). Frankly, I never aspired to be a minister's wife. There was enough commitment to assume that role, but could I measure up to the expectations of a pluralistic congregation? More important, could anyone meet my expectations of an ideal minister? It certainly was not exciting news when Bob began to feel the call of God to a church-related vocation. As I look back, it was an early testing of my faith in God's process as opposed to my desires. As faith is the evidence of things not seen, I accepted (reluctantly, at first) Bob's interpretation of God's leadership in his life—hoping it would strengthen and stimulate my own commitment.

I taught and ministered to a group of sixth-grade girls in a Sunday School class. Active in women's missionary education and Church Training classes were a normal part of my involvement. Visiting members and prospective members required additional time and attention. Oh, I'm not saying that I was any busier than any other minister's wife. I am saying mine was a busy and fulfilling life, and I loved it! Just as it was demanding, it was rewarding —both emotionally and spiritually. Many members of the congregation helped me to become a whole person, one of life's encompassing goals.

The mystery of each new day kept life exciting and full. But one day my tensions began to mount as peculiar health symptoms appeared. I was assisting in the church office, working with figures. Accuracy was primary. But this presented no problem since my training and business experience were secretarial and accounting.

Suddenly I experienced double and triple images. Surely, a cup of strong coffee and a rest of my eyes would correct this annoyance. One of the ladies noted some bookkeeping discrepancies and jokingly chided, "Opha, looks like you have reached the age that forces us to wear glasses." We all laughed although mine was a nervous giggle. The multiple vision persisted.

I was sure a quick visit to our ophthalmologist friend would correct this vision problem. Upon completing the examination, he said, "Opha, your eyes are in good condition, and you do not need glasses. Perhaps the muscles are tired from overuse in the detailed work required for bookkeeping." What a relief!

I dismissed the matter only to find the vision flare-ups came intermittently and unrelated to office work. Often, before I could get to the doctor's office, they would subside, but my concern increased. Something was just not right.

Time moved along quickly with the interchange of friends and family. The vision returned to normal, but limb extremities were tingling and numb. A drug prescription would probably take care of the imagined circulation problem. As it persisted, I visited our family internal physician. His examination indicated no circulation problem. But his diagnosis did not relieve the tingling nor my increasing concern about the strange things that were happening to my body.

Maybe these body irregularities are normal for the developmental process of persons in the mid-thirties. (Bob once said that I was "middle-aged." Of course I corrected him and claimed to be a "young adult." Since then, he has learned never to call a lady "middle-aged," no matter what her age may be!)

One day we were having a family picnic in the park. Good food, ants, good fun playing games, and all that goes with picnics. The fun ended when my limbs failed to respond while gliding off the end of the high slide. As I slumped on the ground, the extremes of emotions came together in a frantic clash. Bob and the girls laughed. I wanted to cry, but didn't. (Mothers try to be brave in front of their children.) A much deeper emotion was stirring in my psyche: this, another incident of my physical disability. Although I tried to make a joke of my legs getting tangled up in the full skirt of the day, I knew my muscles did not respond to my need. What was going to happen next?

After other similar indicators, I found myself at the office of the orthopedist. After his examination and x rays of the lower spine and upper thigh, we felt relieved to hear him say, "Everything looks fine, Mrs. Bingham." The thought came to me, *Everything may look fine, but everything is not fine!*

In spite of the diagnosis, things did improve. But you can imagine my surprise when all of the above symptons returned at the same time with more intensity. In addition, I was having an imbalance problem. Obviously, the time had come when I must face some neurological tests. Talk about anxiety! Going to a "nerve doctor" is a whole different ball game than eye, bone, and general doctors. Frightening adjectives like "traumatic," "threatening," and "debilitating" came to my mind.

After a week of exhaustive hospital neurological testing with myelograms, encephalograms, and spinal taps, the neurologist came to my bed to announce that as soon as my splitting headache subsided I could go home. His diagnosis was fragmented to a patient who wanted to hear absolutes. "Something is wrong with your nervous system, but we find no tumor." I guess that should be counted as good news. But all of those peculiar sensations did not leave. Getting released from the hospital was only short-term relief. I wanted a whole functioning body again.

Leaving the hospital gave me a growing awareness of why the medical profession uses the expression "the practice of medicine." They, too, are practicing in the arena of life. I had previously felt doctors could find the answer for every medical problem. Yet even modern technology often renders them helpless to make proof-positive diagnoses. (Later we were to learn that multiple sclerosis was a classic disease in this mysterious category.) In spite of repositioning my doctor friends from the ethereal heights of "Godlike" to human-limitations, we still thanked God for dedicated technically trained people in the disciplined professions of medical science.

Life seemed to return to normal. Days began to fill with activities that brought a deep sense of pride and worth. Bob had accepted an invitation to serve the Wieuca Road Baptist Church in Atlanta, Georgia. There was excitement in the move although we regretted leaving Greenville, our church friends, and our medical community. We did not know any physicians in Atlanta. How would we adjust in a new city if the pieces of my medical problem did not fall into shape? This query became a matter of faith, a condition of life that would continually be put to the test in the remaining years of my life.

On the day the moving van came to pack our furniture, I had planned a fun-day lawn party for my Sunday School class. Imagine the scene: playing active yard games with the girls, giving instructions to the movers, and silently wondering if my muscles, eyesight, and imbalance would betray me. That evening was consumed with the farewell reception at the church and driving to Atlanta. Not just an ordinary drive! The new interstate highway was under construction. Our girls were weepy over leaving their little friends. Enroute our headlights shorted out about midnight, and we trailed a truck into Atlanta arriving about 2:00 AM. As we pulled into our new driveway, I remember saying, "If I can survive a day like this, there's nothing of consequence wrong with me." The words *multiple sclerosis* had not yet passed through my ears, lips, or brain. I had no reason to know the patterns of remission and exacerbation that were to become a norm for my life.

Remission continued for the first year in Atlanta. There were few idle moments as we adjusted and related to a new congregation, new school, neighborhood, and city. Maybe I had weathered the storm. Surely, the Lord had intervened to bring physical stability back to me.

But shortly without warning, my coordination and equilibrium became obviously noticeable. I said to Bob, "I will be terribly embarrassed if our church members see me swaying as I walk." Bob's words of encouragement usually had a practical implication along with his moral support. "Honey, people who know you recognize that drinking is not your problem. Those who don't know you don't care." But like any recurring problem, it increased in my perception and began to derail me from the areas of life where I wanted to be involved.

The flood of unanswered questions resurfaced and sent us seeking further medical opinions. As God has walked with us through our entire pilgrimage, he was present again to provide a noted neurosurgeon within our church fellowship. After several days of physically exhaustive and mentally draining tests, the doctor shared with us the classic MS diagnostic dilemma: "Opha, I am pleased to say that we find no evidence of a tumor or aneurysm. However, there is evidence that you have some disorder in your central nervous system. There are some indications that it may be multiple sclerosis."

He gave Bob some books written in lay language and suggested that I read only the amount of information that seemed best for my emotions at the moment. (Several months later, Bob gave me the books to read for myself.) I was glad I didn't have to read the dismal predictions of MS. They were couched in words of gloom and uncertainty, phrased in concepts that included no known cause or remedy. One book stated the only hope for the patient was long-term remission or the possibility of a breakthrough in research.

Evidently, the author was discounting the presence and grace of God. Without his impact in my life I had little hope indeed. Subconsciously, I felt the symptoms of MS would disappear— either medically treated or miraculously cured. Why not? I had the best professional care available plus the spiritual care of a loving Heavenly Father.

Time moved along; neither of these support systems seemed to bring remission to the strange, unpredictable muscle reactions of my body. The neurosurgeon suggested we see a neurologist.

The next day found us in the office of a neurologist. He examined my medical record, made some routine tests, and pronounced with an unusual degree of certainty, "Mrs. Bingham, I am sorry to tell you that you have . . . MULTIPLE SCLEROSIS!" We were not faced with the certainty of such long-term illness and disability until now. This moment seemed like an eternity as the depth of meaning raced through our thoughts. We were brought back to reality when the doctor continued his findings by prognosticating, "My judgment is that your disability will increase steadily. You will probably be confined to a wheelchair within two years."

My state of mental shock probably allowed me to disregard my childhood training to respect professional people and their opinions. I blurted out, "Not me! I refuse to accept no other alternative than being immobilized in two years." His words of restating the problem and futile attempt to soften his prognosis were falling on deaf ears. Perhaps he did me a great favor. Pussyfooting around the issue might have lulled me into a state of self-pity and pathos.

Bob and I made a habit of dining out together immediately following a visit to the doctor's office. This particular luncheon was a milestone in our relationship to one another of positioning ourselves to the challenge at hand. We decided what we would say to the girls, to the church, to genuinely interested friends, to polite inquirers. We set some short- and long-range goals for ourselves and the family. Most important of all: without reservation, we committed our lives again into the hands of him who created us and has the power to keep us. (As you continue to read you will see the importance of these goals and how we worked to achieve them amidst many unplanned and frightening situations.)

Then began the series of "why" questions. These are some time-honored questions that have tried the souls of human beings for hundreds of years. But they become intensely personal when you become the asker and the answerer. The non-Christian sees them as rhetorical or rebellious questions. The Christian addresses them reverently. The pursuing of the answer leads us into a closer walk with our Creator.

"Why" questions are basically theologically oriented. It is only as we struggle with God in a Jacobian manner that we find eternal answers. It is an encounter with life-or-death stakes when our cultural Christian veneer is skinned off to the bone. In this painful process, we internalize answers that sustain sanity when life is at its nadir.

The first such question was one common to humankind: "WHY did this happen to me? Why me?" I had been a Christian since my earliest recollection. Believing in the teachings came easy, and I wanted to act like my Master. Active in church and community ministry was not a duty but a pleasure. Seldom did the sun set on an unforgiven sin. Why me?

During those early years I would come to some understanding, only to face the resurfacing of the same question again and again. Was there no satisfactory answer? Was God playing games with me? What was the point of this cat-and-mouse exercise reappearing on the video screen of my soul and mind?

2
Searching for a Prescription

How do you begin to find answers for a disease that even medical science finds baffling? It can be more frustrating than searching for the proverbial needle in a haystack. (At least you know for what you are looking.) Alas, with all the modern research done on MS, the medical profession does not know what causes it or how to arrest it. Yet failing to search for some answer would be the beginning of giving in to pessimism and despair.

Our search took us to the Library of Congress. Their helpfulness was only exceeded by the lack of printed material for the nonmedical person. While it has stacks of volumes on the medical and technical aspects of MS, there were less than a dozen books listed on how to live with long-term illnesses.

Sometimes the family needs more facts about the disease than the patient. This could be true in the early stages when I did not want to face up to the facts. The depth and interpretation of the information should fit the maturity of the family member. Bob could absorb more information than I, and I more than our small children. But we all need some facts to counterbalance the mystery of noninformation and misinformation. Patient and family alike: we all live in a fourth world reserved for the handicapped.

Strange but true, each family member needs to make an independent and private diagnosis of the case. Hopefully, it is based on sound medical advice tempered with God's wisdom. Likewise, family members must be willing to alter their prognosis depending upon the case history and upon their faith.

Most everyone has had an acquaintance who has died with cancer or perhaps a drastic heart ailment. But how many MS patients have you known well enough to speak openly about coping with MS? Articles are found almost daily in our newspapers on other debilitating illnesses. Most MS articles deal with continuing research being done in the hope to isolate the cause. What I am trying to say is that it is not easy to find answers. In order to identify with other patients and their families, I have listed my physical, emotional, and spiritual pilgrimages in search for a prescription to cope with a lifelong illness.

My story necessarily relates to MS, but its scope extends to any long-term illness or handicap. While the case study may be specific in nature, it is general in application. Where one is in a life/death struggle for who knows how long, what difference does the cause of the struggle make? Call it MS, lupus, cancer, or any one of many illnesses. Call it paraplegic or quadriplegic. Call it by Latin names, anglicized names, or common names. Call it what you want. If you expect to take it with you to your grave, they all have a common parenthood.

Each of us brings a particular set of problems and needs to apply to the reading of this book. Yet all of us have a common set of problems and needs. If you are a patient, you want answers on how to live in spite of consequences. If you are family or friends, you want answers on how to relate to the patient. Our commonality is not the medical rootage of our problems. That is the area we refer to medically trained professions of stethoscope, sutures, and test tubes. Our commonality is the emotional fact that life must go on. How it goes on and how we adjust to its new patterns is our common rootage.

Physical

We began to read anything we could find in print. Medical journals, MS bulletins, and less professionally researched articles in the *Reader's Digest* and the airlines in-flight magazines. Friends often sent us clippings from everywhere. Solutions varied from extensive laboratory research to reports using snake venom. We did not consider any information as ridiculous, but neither did we shuffle off to Buffalo for experimentation. Here are some of the steps we took in the physiological prescription search.

● *Annual visit to the doctor.*—While he was always attentive and gave me the regular battery of office neurological tests, the visit was primarily supportive. A highly skilled person is looking after my physical welfare. He keeps abreast of the research. He knows my medical history and writes prescriptions accordingly. This periodic check is supportive during the rest of the year when I am not in his office.

● *Swimming.*—Early on I went to the local family YMCA for swimming. The instructors were sensitive to my progressively weak muscles. The hour in the pool was enjoyable by getting to meet new persons, plus having a morning out of the house. After several months this pleasant experience turned into another dead end. Just getting from the house to the pool was so exhausting. After arriving, all I could do was hang on to the side of the pool with little energy left for exercising my legs. Realizing that I needed enough energy to drive the two miles back to our home, I found a new use for my raincoat even on a sunny day. When there was not enough energy to dress completely, the raincoat was easy to slip over the wet swimsuit.

● *Hospital retesting.*—Five years after the original diagnosis, our physician suggested we retake the neurological tests for verification. When seriously considering what life might hold in the next twenty or more years with MS, we secretly hoped the tests would locate a tumor, so it could surgically be removed. The possibility of it being cancerous paled in the possibility of being crippled and helpless until death. Fortunately, no tumor was discovered. Unfortunately, the previous diagnosis was verified.

● *Contact with MS Society.*—This has been positive and supportive. It began with a chance meeting of a field representative with the national society. Working out of the Norfolk, Virginia, office he kept us informed of any new discoveries. He assured us in 1971 that any day the doctors would have the answer to this mystifying disease. Promises, promises! But that was all he could offer. Meanwhile, we received the periodic editions of *Mile Stones,* Georgia Chapter, National Multiple Sclerosis Society magazine.

● *Medication.*—Reports were printed that some people were receiving miraculous relief from certain medicines. My doctor prescribed some of these, but none seemed to meet my needs. The steroids initially were very helpful, so helpful that one day my hopes were sent flying. Normal mobility had returned! I drove to the shopping center and purposely parked in the space fartherest from the stores just to prove to myself I could walk. The sheer joy of walking normal again brought such delight. This emotional high was short-lived. The mind was willing, the determination was strong, but my body chemistry soon rejected the steroids.

New "cures" appear on the horizon regularly. They always claim some promise but seem to fade away, hopefully harmlessly. Recently the *New England Journal of Medicine* reported a scientific testing of increased oxygen with an increased barometric pressure. We read each page with care and scrutinized the statistical results. In consultation with physicians, we concluded that the positive effects were limited to patients with a short-term history and continuing increase of symptoms. Finally, we felt this treatment was not for me. Was it lack of faith? Was it a mistake not to experiment? Was it wise to wait for further validation of the experiment? Maybe I'll know in a few years. Maybe not.

Maybe I am waiting on a miracle that will never come. Or the miracle has already come, and I failed to recognize it. Or the adversaries of FAITH and SCIENCE are playing out their roles in my life through mutual patterns, albeit indistinguishable ones. And if that miracle of total healing appears, will I even care which agent played the greatest part. I want to be healed and walk again. Philosophical jousting of faith and science are not my first priority. (Hope that doesn't bother you!) Long-term illnesses tend to change one's perspective from fantasy to realism. If you wish to make this an issue of faith, so be it—read on to see how such matters are reconciled in the crucible of life!

In a rare moment of subjectivity our doctor one day mused,

"The only reliable prescription is that the spouse and family give an abundance of love and support to the patient." Those words have been prophetic.

• *Physical therapy at home.*—While a visiting therapist has come to the house on occasions to give suggestions, the best therapy I have found is refusing to "take to the bed." This one decision probably has been the best medication available. It enables me to continue the housework necessary, on a limited basis, for a comfortable home: meal preparation, sewing, laundry, and ironing along with the multiple chores only a homemaker knows.

Perhaps the greatest challenge has been to make the round trip to our laundry room in the basement: *fourteen long, high steps each way.* Even though it is a twenty-minute exercise in determination, it is so satisfying to know that I can climb my own "mountain." It is noteworthy that the "mountain" was unclimbable until we had a railing installed on each side of the steps. It becomes a toss-up which gets more exercise: legs or arms.

• *Walking aids.*—Beginning with Bob's arm, the aids progressed to a walking cane, a three-pronged cane, a walker, and now a wheelchair for distances longer than fifty feet—and always while traveling. More about this in chapter 7.

• *Yard work.*—While looking for technical therapy, I did not want to overlook the obvious. It was found in our rock garden. The flashbacks to growing and cultivating flowers were a positive remembrance of childhood. But walking, stooping, climbing, cutting, pruning, watering, sowing, weeding, fertilizing were not barriers to a healthy farm girl. Regardless of the hours spent on tasks that normally require minutes, the rock garden has provided long-lasting physical therapy and lots more fun than calisthenic-type exercises.

General Prescription for Physical Needs: Don't give up the ship! Keep bailing water. It will keep you from drowning, not to mention keeping your spirit toned up. If you become concerned that a breakthrough has come unknown to you, take comfort that such news would soon be voiced in the media around the world.

Emotional

Long-term illness carries different emotional baggage than short-term illness. The very fact that it is diagnosed as an illness that will extend into many years makes it different and more difficult, particularly if the odds are good that you will carry it to your grave.

Short-term illness is fearsome in its own right. Often it is dramatic, coming to a crisis with the speed of a thunderstorm. It may strike with lightening damage even unto death. But it also may pass over as a storm that moves quickly off the horizon. In a few months one forgets that it passed that way.

Perhaps the greatest emotional struggle has been dealing with the medical fact that MS is not curable at this time. Dead myelin cannot be restored except by divine intervention of re-creation. If only the doctor could prescribe some sure-cure medicine. Or a surgeon could extricate diseased tissue and replace with a transplant. Maybe a "muscle maker" could do for me what a pacemaker does for thousands of heart patients today. I would not mind extensive treatments that extended through months if I had some assurance that the disease would be arrested—not to mention that it might be cured.

Then there is the frustration of giving the appearance of not being seriously ill. Casual acquaintances may not recognize any noticeable symptoms of illness. You hear comments like, "You look so good. Have you been cured?" It is not that you seek attention or pity. It is that people come to expect normal activities from you which your weakened body is incapable of delivering. People unthinkingly walk briskly off from you in a crowd, expecting you to be close by. Sometimes you may feel like shouting, "Hey, remember my mobility is limited!"

Naturally the presence of a walker or wheelchair abates the problem. But most handicapped persons want to get those aids out of sight as much as possible. When sitting at the dinner table, all of a sudden your hand cannot grasp the fork and food drops on your clothing. An understanding friend says nothing. But what is the new acquaintance thinking? You cannot wear a sign around your neck announcing, "I have MS, and my muscles are not functioning well today."

The mental health I bring to the disease is predictably the mental health that I can expect to keep throughout the course of the illness. This has been my observation of other patients also. It is true that crises often bring out the worst or best in a person. It may be more predictable that one's mental attitudes are actually extended and accented through crisis.

Mental attitudes are directly proportional to how positively I am involved in ministering to others. I can be singing the blues in a minor key. One visit with Bob to a shut-in will change my tune and set my attitude in a major key. One advantage to being handicapped is that people usually do not expect as much from you. When you exert normal efforts to serve them, the effort is perceived out of proportion, particularly if you carry out your mission on a rainy day. They think you have been sent through the clouds from heaven!

One time I felt unglued. The black shades of life were all drawn. Janet called and asked if we could get together. She was only twenty-six years old, but her MS was progressing at a fearful rate. Janet says our visits are so helpful to her. If she only knew how much they help me! It is like getting a new glue job.

It even works vicariously. When Bob shares my pilgrimage with others, I get the same lift. A Kansas friend of Bob's called the other day to say that their talks had given him a whole new perspective relating to coping with long-term illness. His colleagues later verified that he is a new person. Just think of it: my witness extending that far to a person I have not met.

General prescription for emotional needs: remember, everybody carries a heavy bag of rocks. Put your limitations into perspective with all of the rest of life. You are probably better off than you think.

Spiritual

It is amazing how we take meticulous care of our bodies while neglecting our spiritual health. We exert our energies on a seventy-year, physical life span to the neglect of an eternal one. Those are mighty poor odds!

Spiritual needs must be met daily. Physical food cannot be neglected for a week with one expecting to gorge oneself and catch up for past oversights. It is just as important that we keep in touch daily with our Creator. A weekly visit to your house of worship is commendable. It is far above the average. It will bring life into focus and friends into fellowship. But it will not take the place of daily spiritual sustenance.

I often hear people pray for God to come into their presence and be near them: good intentions, poor theology. God promised always to be near us, closer than a brother. We pray that he will watch over us, and he has promised to constantly care for us. Doesn't he care for the sparrows? Could it be that we are not daily making ourselves aware of his presence? If we read his Word and talk with him daily, indeed we are spiritually fed. While Bob and I daily have devotions, I find myself talking with God countless times each day. One may be shortchanged physically, but no one needs to feel spiritually impoverished.

The frustration and mystery of an unpredictable disease surely deepened my dependence upon God. However, just like healthy persons, I have periods of better physical and mental health than the average. It is easy to take relief from adversity as your "right" rather than a privilege. During these high times, it is more difficult to feel dependent upon God. And as surely as the sun rises in the east, we tend to lose the closeness of God's presence.

Surely, it has been in the quiet times of struggle that we have grown spiritually. Bob has often decried, "It doesn't seem fair that God allows Opha to experience trauma to bring me back to dependency upon him." Who promised life would be fair?

While using my walker at the grocery store, a fellow shopper threw her arms around me saying that she could tell I was a Christian. Taken by surprise, I confirmed that she was right, but how could she tell? "Because you have a special glow, and I can tell you are praising the Lord in your suffering." If she had only known how depleted I was, struggling to get the few items on my list. Some people have made it hard for me to understand about praising God in suffering. They have confused it for me when they say we should praise God "for" our suffering: not me. God did not inflict MS upon me, and I do not praise him because I have MS. But I do praise him for his sustaining grace. However, in chapter 11 I will discuss this in greater length. (It may take you nine chapters to digest this preliminary concept of suffering.)

Faith healing must be dealt with in a long-term illness. I would not limit God to a mortal healer. Neither would I discount the possibility that God can and does work through human instrumentality. I have some friends who claim that they were cured at a healing service. I believe them. I keep seeking God's complete healing grace, but he has chosen not to dispense it for the present.

Here is another of the "why" questions. First, I have answered to some degree of satisfaction, "Why did it happen to me?" Now, I am asking, "Why can't I be cured?" It is a normal question and will recur until I resolve it. (And after that, it may come back in a different form!) My theology is so simple I blush to put it into print. At such a risk, here it is.

1. Has God worked a miracle in your life?
2. If not, why not?
3. Is it because he cannot, or will not?
4. If he cannot, get yourself another God.
5. If he will not, find out why not.
6. Then, what is God's will for my life?
7. How do I respond to his will?

Were these seven brief sentences confusing? Perhaps. They are

trying to capsule a flood of spiritual truths. Have the multiple
"nots" become a literary barrier? They were meant to be bridges
to spiritual barriers. Faith understanding to spiritual acceptance
of suffering may be God's substitution for faith healing. Read the
above seven statements again until you understand the logical
progression. Note that regardless of the responses, the ultimate
question is stated in terms of God's will for our lives.

In proofreading this manuscript, I have relived many years,
many questions, and many pains. Realizing I am not normal and
can't do what others can do, I try to put these feelings out of my
mind, but they surface, finally, like a volcano erupting to get
release. Such release is redemptive but often accompanied with
physical and emotional pain.

Believe me when I say that my spiritual life and attitude is laced
with the recurring question, "Why does God not heal me?" In the
last ten years I think I have found some answers. Hopefully, you
will too.

Friends often ask how meaningful is prayer after twenty-plus
years of MS. Any good book on prayer will give you a systematic
look at the value of conversation with God. Let me list the basis
of my personal prayer life (not my family or corporate prayer life):

1.   Talking-listening in personal conversation with God
2.   Discussing my short-term/long-term needs
3.   Praising God for his goodness each day
4.   Asking forgiveness for my lack of faith
5.   Praying for others specifically according to their needs

Here are some specific events that have driven me to a posture
of prayer. (Years ago I would have used the expression "driven
me to my knees." Since MS, I have learned that disabilities affect
most segments of my life, including the inability to pray on my
knees.) I find prayer the best prescription for the following situations:

1. When I can't function, I sit down and ask for strength to function, or patience to live with my inability.
2. When tempted to give up.
3. When depressed and in need a happy spirit.
4. When I need to praise God rather than complain to him.
5. When blessings are so numerous I can't count them.
6. When I call my faith into question.
7. When my patience with Bob needs long-suffering qualities. Sometimes he thinks he knows more about my needs than I do.
8. When facing hospitalization.
9. When needing extra strength to minister to someone.

A friend composed this prayer for me in 1974. I use her original handwritten copy as I write this segment of the manuscript.

I Prayed Again

I prayed again this morning that your body he would
touch.
And then my mind was filled with Paul and how he prayed so
much.
He asked that God would heal him and set his body free,
And God kept sweetly saying, "My grace is sufficient for
thee."
So, I'll pray again tomorrow that he'll teach me how to
pray,
And I'll place you in his loving care and let him have his
way.
Then I know our faith will strengthen as he leads us by
the hand.
For the Father knows our future, with love He made the plan.
Let us take this grace he promised to folk like you and
me,
And it will be sufficient, for he said that it would be.

MARCELLA RAY

General prescription for spiritual needs: it is vital to know that your spiritual investments have stamped upon them "In God we trust." Spiritual health is maintained by proximity to the Maker of heaven and earth and not with the things that money can buy.

3
Accepting the Condition

Accepting long-term illness is not as rational as the advice to cooperate with the inevitable. Death may be inevitable but the course of MS is unpredictable. How then do you make peace with uncertainty?

First, reduce and minimize the variables. Second, isolate the irreducible minimums so you can objectify them. Third, come to a decision what you intend to do about them. As an example, one variable is the possibility of total lack of ambulation. Does that mean I can still use a wheelchair? Or will someone need to attend the chair? In either case, what restrictions will that have on my life-style? How will it affect the basic priorities? Will I look upon the wheelchair as a friend or foe? What modifications need to be made in our home, yard, or auto to make this adjustment as convenient as possible?

When it began to sink in that I actually had one of the feared long-term illnesses, I tried to determine what general reaction I would make. Would it be to withdraw from life and wither? Or would it be to accept it and adjust? Looking at these options on paper today, they seem so simple. But believe me, they represent the poles of options. The various degrees of choice between the poles became the battleground of tough decisions.

Mentally I considered all the deviants to my former active life-style and tried to accept MS as a challenge to be attacked and, hopefully, conquered. Again, the multiple challenges are grouped in the same three familiar categories: physical, emotional, and spiritual.

Physical

Seeing no benefit in living in constant fear, I decided to face the changes as realistically as possible. Well-meaning friends made withdrawal a tempting option. "Oh, Mrs. Bingham, why are you using a cane?" "You seem to be dragging your leg." "It has taken a long time for your leg to return to normal." "Opha, what is really wrong with you?"

At first it was so difficult to respond to them. Did they really want to know? Was their inquiry more related to "Hello, how are you?" Should I tell them the diagnosis? If so, how much information did they want to know? I was tempted to shrug and say, "Oh, guess I am not as bouncy as I used to be."

After a few months of that "cat-and-mouse game" I decided they might as well know the truth, and handle it the best way they could. But it was hard to get the two words out of my mouth: *multiple sclerosis.* Our younger daughter, Nancy, unknowingly helped at this point. (We had told the girls early on.) She was seven years old and had some difficulty pronouncing six strange syllables. If she were not so serious about it, it might have been downright humorous. I decided if Nancy could get those words out of her throat and past her front teeth, so could I. Giant step for Opha.

When people would inquire about my disability, I would try to determine if they were curious, polite, or concerned. If curious, my response might be, "I have some muscle problems, and I'm getting along fairly well." If polite, perhaps I'd say, "I have MS and seem to be making it better than the doctor predicted." If genuinely concerned, I would take time to give them a brief history, diagnosis, and progress and encourage their questions. It did not take too long to realize the curious and polite did not want to struggle with my problems any more than I wanted to share them. But to share with a concerned friend brought release from a feeling of loneliness amidst the struggle—a lifelong struggle.

To deny a person any degree of independence is to force some degree of incarceration. Would I become a captive in my own house? Little did I know how prophetic that question would become in later years. Not until the last few years have we owned two autos. This meant that our one automobile was not readily available for my use. Although I can drive with certain limitations, Bob usually needed the car for business which left me stranded at home. My "castle" was transformed into a "prison," no way to get down the steep driveway to get the daily mail delivery, no means of driving to a weekday meeting at the church. When Bob was out of town and used the car, my condition was nearing solitary confinement. No one was keeping me in, but there was hardly a way to get out. When we recognized what was happening, we managed to keep our old car at the time we bought a new one. Free at last!

Whose captive would I become? Would disease and illness hold the keys to my life? Or would it be fear? Or steps? Or lonesomeness? What about being considered only a partial person?

But there are some potential positive captors in life. Maybe I could choose to be their captive if I must be at times dependent and restricted. Maybe I could be a true servant to the needs of others. I might continue to give myself unrelentingly to my family and feel I had a part in their lives. When all was said and done, thought and rethought, weighed and reweighed, I chose to continue to be a servant for Jesus Christ. This seemed to encompass all of the positive choices. Likewise, it would help me to overcome the negative options.

Like many mountaintop experiences, the reality of the valley comes quickly. Frustration bore deeply into my consciousness when I could not do the countless physical chores needed to be done in a day's work. Being "handicapped" was more than an expression: it was a constant burden.

God is always looking after his children. This was never more evident than in our selection of our new house in Atlanta. It was just one year prior to final diagnosis when we moved from Greenville. We knew something was wrong with my body, but we expected it to be treated and eventually to disappear. In looking for a house, we never gave any consideration to seeking out one having qualities that would be barrier free. We told the real estate lady that our house priorities were for a level, tree-studded lot, a den with fireplace, and room arrangement that we could live in and could afford. We prayed that God would provide our house according to his wisdom.

It came as a surprise. The lot was (and is, for after twenty-three years we still live here) very hilly, had no trees or a fireplace. But it may be one of the few houses in Atlanta that you can walk directly from the driveway into the kitchen or den without even one riser! We planted almost one hundred pine seedlings on the hill and had a fireplace built in the den. But God provided the barrier-free entrance when we had no foreknowledge of its necessity.

Little irritants tend to prick one to pieces. Like giving up collecting for worthy fund-raising campaigns in the neighborhood. I missed talking with the friends in the nearby homes. I missed the satisfaction of accomplishing something of intrinsic worth. Then one day it hit me: not only can I not collect for the heart fund, the cancer fund, polio, and the like, I am an indirect recipient for the MS drive. (While never receiving any direct compensation, I have realized the hope that comes from the research being done.)

Then there was the adjustment to using a wheelchair. The very thought of using that "rolling casket" was objectionable to most of my senses. To accept its invitation for accommodation was to "give in." I refused to do so. And what happened? I stayed home when I could have been out and about. I missed out on some social events. I labored unnecessarily for ambulation of long distances that robbed me of energy for nonambulation tasks. (You may have noticed the overusage of the first person pronoun in this paragraph. This was designed. My basic problem with the wheelchair was an ego one. I did not want to be known as an "invalid.") Once I could accept the chair as an ally, it was easy to accept other aids.

Making peace with other aids about the house somehow was

easier. We determined to keep our home from looking like an institution. A little creativity helped. The grab bars in the closets are out of sight. The bars in the bathtub are covered with attractive towels. The bedside commode sets in a chair designed and built to match the other furniture in the room. And naturally, the collapsible wheelchair still stays out of sight since it is used exclusively for out-of-the-home trips.

General physical acceptance: face up to the truth. It is easier than you think. Physical limitations do not a prison make.

Emotional

You probably noted in the above section that there is some overlap between the physical and the emotional. You will see this also evident in this section as well as the spiritual arena. We humans are holistic in nature and therefore difficult to segmentize.

Emotional security is a must for me to function. My emotions were stable prior to the diagnosis. But the likelihood of long-term illness seemed to put me on the track of a roller coaster. Temporary though it was, it was frightening. My husband seemed to become the balance wheel to help me tick. By giving support when needed and constructive criticism when necessary, he was my catalyst for restablizing my emotions.

We established some quality time for caring, sharing, and demonstrating our love. We decided on a weekly luncheon date. A casual hour taken from his busy schedule and my isolation. Since the dates were set in our calendars each January, there had to be some substitutions and a few cancellations. It was therapy thrice experienced. I looked forward to it, enjoyed the moment, and relived it several days following.

Little things mean a lot when you have long periods of time to contemplate them. Of unusual pleasure has been playing a game of cribbage with Bob after our evening meal. He had been playing competitively with a friend for several years and always looked forward to his weekly games. But he seemed to just tolerate playing with me. I asked him one day why he did not seem excited about playing cribbage with me. He frankly told me that since I did not care about winning, he did not care about playing. Since that time I have become a tiger at cribbage.

Perhaps my greatest fear was the potential loss of sexual satisfaction. Fourteen years of unusual compatibility had been rewarding. But what about the next twenty to thirty years? One of the early symptoms of MS was the malfunction of my hips. Accompanying that was the loss of feeling in my uterus area. I can recall the rejection of the thought of being thirty-six years old and having little, if any, sexual gratification!

It was during this trauma that it became obvious that love making was a combination of physical, emotional, and spiritual factors. For a few months it was necessary to minimize the physical factor. In doing so, it was so obvious that God meant for his children to love above the level of animals. Marriage is indeed a union, and the sex act is a living symbol of two individuals who have become one. But intercourse is only a symbol of a deeper emotional and spiritual experience of being one together. Perhaps it was only coincidental that when we came to understand this truth that the hip and pelvic malfunctions subsided. And we have lived and loved happily ever after! (In fact, I never imagined in those younger years that a couple approaching sixty years of age could possibly enjoy sex.)

Several years later Bob came home and was unusually bubbling with excitement. He said he had an unusual Christmas gift for me this year. After teasing me with the possibilities and raising my inquisitive level out of sight, he said he had made arrangements for a vasectomy. You male readers will never know how much that meant to me at that moment and ever after. The fear of late pregnancy vanished! But much more, it gave me the ultimate emotional security that my husband loved me as much as he loved himself. Ladies, I can assure you that such selflessness on the part of your mate covers up multitudes of petty thoughtlessness.

There were other emotional adjustments to be faced.

● Friends and secondary family members who either did not understand or overresponded in their desire to help.

● The need to become more independent and aggressive in most matters other than physically related.

● How to respond to the innocent-but-uninformed encourager who tries to relate by saying that an aunt died with MS after a long and painful illness.

● Taking a group of sixth graders from our church to sing carols for a neighbor lady who had MS. This was my first glimpse of a person showing the ravages of muscle deterioration. It was difficult at that moment to sing "Joy to the World." But I did. (Twenty years later I was to experience the joy of church and Girl Scout groups coming to sing carols to me. Two groups came last night while I was reading the manuscript.)

● Trying to seek a balance between risking physical impairment or risking emotional depression. We decided it was better to try to walk down the steep driveway and risk a broken hip than to become depressed by forced incarceration in the house.

● Since Bob travels extensively, should I retool all the locks and security devices? Complain about his absence? Have a lady friend spend the nights with me or just be scared to death? Fortunately, I chose to seek a longtime friend, a single working lady, when I needed a companion. She has become a very special person in my life: like a sister. Talk about unexpected benefits: if I had been well these years, she and I would not have had an opportunity to become soul sisters. During these extended periods together, she takes me to the stores to shop and to church functions. I prepare her breakfast and evening meals giving me a sense of accomplishment and worth.

● Should I make necessity the mother of invention, or should I play on people's sympathy to get what I wanted?

General emotional acceptance: emotional security begins with your loved ones and ends with your loved ones. In between are the misty flats that may send you to and fro.

Spiritual

Most solutions to our physical and emotional problems are based upon spiritual understandings. Trained scholars tend to call this a systematic theology. While that is deep water for me to wade, I do remember Karl Barth's response to the press interview. When asked what was the basis of his theological understanding, he replied, "Jesus loves me! this I know, For the Bible tells me so."

Following that profound but simple statement, my acceptance to living with MS is related to trying to understand the depth of God's love for me. The original pressing question was, "Why did God allow this to happen?"

Through the years it changed to: "There must be a reason for God to show his love in this fashion." Then, "How can he trust me so much to be his witness under stressing circumstances?"

Never fear: Satan was busy doing his thing while I was muddling through an acceptance of God's love. There was the temptation to reason: if God really loved me, why does he allow me to be handicapped? Again, the temptation came to think that God saw me as less than a whole person and that I was being punished for some sins of the past. Oh, Job, where are you? And the temptation brought from my friends that if I just had enough faith, I would be cured. Oh, Job's friends, where are you?

There seems to be a struggle between fatalism, realism, and faith. Fatalism has its inherent depression; realism has its accompanying starkness; faith has its intermittent disappointment due to our seeing "in a mirror dimly" (1 Cor. 13:12, RSV). Yet it was my recognition that only spiritual values are eternal that helped me to accept my incurable physical condition.

Do you want to read a spiritual high? Here's one: realizing that one day I will meet my Master face-to-face . . . in a perfect spiritual body!

General spiritual acceptance: This world is not my home; I'm only limping through. But God is walking close beside me.

4
Determining the Course

How do you navigate in the fourth world—the world in which handicapped persons find themselves? To some degree it is an uncharted area. Better stated, each person must become the navigator of her own ship. Not in the tradition of *Invictus:*

> I am the master of my fate;
> I am the captain of my soul.

That type-minded person may well find herself floundering on the rocks and shoals of hopelessness rather than in the tradition of a navigator willing to follow the commands of the Master.

Basically, this is a decision to act rather than react. It is easy for a handicapped person to take the line of least resistance. But this puts all the initiative on someone else. It sounds tempting at first. We leave the responsibility to others. If things don't turn out right—well, it's their fault. The long-term problem surfaces that you no longer have control of your life: by the hour, the day, the year, or forever. Another form of loss of freedom.

I am not a liberating revolutionary by nature. (Those who know me will be belly laughing at this point.) I am somewhat reserved but determined to be more independent when I begin to chart the course for the rest of my life with long-term illness. Somewhere, I heard that you cannot control a ship that is dead in the water. It must be moving before it can be steered. Of course, by acting I risk being off course, having a collision, or going aground. But at least I am not "dead" in my pilgrimage. I do have some steerage, some control. Thank God for making us free agents, independent to choose for ourselves.

General Direction

● We set our priorities: putting first things first. Since Bob and I are on this journey together, we spent a week at the beach in 1961 to get some perspective. While the girls were frolicking and surfing, we were reading the Sermon on the Mount, again and again. Each reading gave us additional insight. We came to the conclusion that we wanted to put God first, our family second, our church third, and everything else would have to compete for priority as the situation demanded.

Some committed Christians may have a problem with priorities number two and three above. So did we. Earlier in our ministry when I was whole and healthy, Bob interchanged these two priorities. I could take care of our young daughters and his mother in our home. He gave his energies without reserve to the work of the church. But when my strength weakened, and the girls grew into puberty, we found that our family operated better when he gave us more support. Incidentally, we now believe his leadership in the church was strengthened in direct proportion to the well-being of our family.

Does this place us outside the high wall of acceptable orthodoxy? We think not. Our basic loyalty is with God, the Three-in-One. We continue to love and serve his church. But we find no Scripture basis for putting the work of the church ahead of the welfare of our family.

● We would rule MS and not let it rule us. To act otherwise would make us a slave to the disease. Obviously, I cannot control the effect of MS on my body. But I was determined to control my reaction and responses.

● We set some challenging but achievable goals. Included were these: (1) Witness in our neighborhood and community by our Christian life-style to the faith, hope, and love of God. (2) Take a family vacation each year with a specific purpose of becoming involved in missions. (3) Keep our home a vibrant and happy place where our friends and the girls' companions would feel welcome. (4) Financially support the girls through college. (5) Provide a wedding service of their choice befitting a Christian family.

● Seek out other persons with long term-illnesses and encourage them. This was not totally selfless. We knew that our lives would be blessed as we sought to serve others. This proved to be prophetic. You will note many incidents of this as you read through the book.

● Continue to live as normal and creative a life as possible. Before MS, people would comment on our personal and family life-style. We did not have abundant economic resources. (Our total income the year I was diagnosed was only $9,400 including our housing allowance.) But we did try to capitalize on our human assets and multiply them by God's abundant resources. This we determined to do as my disease progressed, and my physical resources were depleted.

● Face problems one day at a time, not borrowing trouble on the future. Look for the positive hope that lies nestled in every cloud. So much has been written on living one day at a time. It's not new. Jesus taught it. I have practiced it or at least made a conscious effort to do so. Every morning when I get up I see this Ralph Waldo Emerson quote in my kitchen:

> What lies behind us
> And what lies before us
> Are tiny matters compared to
> What lies within us.

● Find ways of turning our apparent disadvantage into an advantage. Adversity can make or break a person. Reinhold Neibuhr phrased it for me when he penned, "God, give us grace to accept with serenity the things that cannot be changed, courage to change things which should be changed, and the wisdom to distinguish the one from the other."

Physical Restraints

Keeping my body as fit as possible is a biblical imperative. It also is an asset to the handicapped. While MS can attack any muscle of the body, it seldom attacks all of the muscles. Therefore, I set out to eat sensibly and keep extra weight from becoming a barrier. This has been an asset through the years, especially now when I must use the walker in the house and the wheelchair for distance when away from the house. Bob has been able to wheel me to almost unreachable places because I weigh just under one hundred pounds, normal weight for my height.

By carrying out the functions of a homemaker I am able to use and exercise many of my muscles. It takes much longer to achieve a household task than formerly. But it does help to keep much of the tone in my muscles plus the fact that it is a tremendous morale builder to be a participant in our family needs.

One of my "no-no's" is **no bed in the daytime.** There are precious few hours to achieve my objectives for the day. If I lie down for awhile, the temptation might be too great to remain in bed. Relaxing in a chair provides relief and recuperation for my tired muscles. To strengthen my eye muscles, I tried to increase my reading habits. Obviously, this brings me into contact with the broader horizon of the world with which I have limited exposure.

Not to be overlooked is the effort to keep abreast of MS in general. After the first few years it was not intimidating to read case studies and medical findings. Annual visits to the neuro specialist, the internal medicine specialist, and the physical therapist were so helpful in making sure our medical sights were on course.

Emotionally

It was like receiving pardon and parole when I recognized that everyone has a handicap or two. Mine happened to be quite obvious. Even that had its advantages since I was forced to face up to it. The journey from abnormal to normal may not be very long, but it is important.

Everyone must relate to certain emotions: love, hate, joy, sorrow, hope, fulfillment, regret, success, failure, fear, rejection, affirmation, loneliness, fellowship, happiness, pity, and a laundry list of others. To one degree or another I will mention these through the book. But several bear attention in this chapter.

● Fear.—This emotion strikes at the mainsail of the physically handicapped. There is the fear of being unprotected, being deserted, being destitute, being alone, being bedfast. But to a lesser degree, does not everyone have these intrusions into a serene life? Perhaps the final decision not to give in to fear came when a builder offered to rekey and put new locks and bolts on every outside door in our house. For me to accept his generous offer would have been giving in to fear. This is not my course.

● Loneliness.—Admittedly, it often becomes lonely in the house since the girls have established their own homes. Bob travels often for the Home Mission Board of the Southern Baptist Convention, and this leaves many days without personal contact with others. Usually, Bob telephones during his lunch hour and often while out of town. Friends call and sometimes stop by. But to overcome the feeling of loneliness when strength is depleted, one must take the initiative.

The loving companionship of Christ's presence is a faithful deterrent to loneliness. Finding companionship in daily prayer, meditation, and Bible study is stimulating to mind and soul. It may seem ritual and routine for you. But without this touch with God, my days would become like a Robinson Crusoe experience without his man Friday.

Then too, I do not expect people to always accommodate my desires. Why wait for them to call and ask me to lunch when it is just as normal for me to initiate the invitation. They usually must drive and handle the wheelchair. But I am the host and receive an additional blessing by getting out of the house.

● Joy.—It is to be found in the little things of life: a thank-you note, remembering a pleasant evening at the symphony, a vacation spot, a daughter phoning to say hello, a granddaughter's first word, having enough house money to finish out the month, preparing homemade rolls for a neighbor, grooming and clipping the ivy on the wall, having a former Sunday School girl call from the airport, winning a game of cribbage with Bob. In all of life, I have purposed to linger with the joys and let the hurts and sorrows disappear into the sunset.

● Love.—Since God is love, then he must have breathed a generous portion of it into his children. No malady can keep us from loving one another. Oh, don't get me wrong; I do not like everything I see or everyone I know. But no one can keep me from loving them. Love is therapeutic and not to be compared with anything else. It begins with loving God, myself, my husband, our daughters, family, and friends. It ends with loving those who do not love us.

How can one manifest such love with physical limitations? Easy. Share a smile rather than a frown, a laugh rather than a groan, a giving spirit rather than a greedy one. These build my own spirit as well as enhance the society around me.

● Pity.—It is a pity that pity is to be pitied. Whereas the word had noble birthing and warm usage, we tend to shun the offer of it. I want your care and concern, your prayers, your offers of help. But I seek not your pity, for it has overtones of a judgment that I cannot overcome my handicap. And I know that I have and can again. Neither do I want MS to be the topic of conversation every time we meet. There is so much more of interest to talk about and about which something can be done. Pity: thanks, but no thanks.

Family

One of the primary and prolonged questions to race through my mind is, "How will this affect my family?" My lifelong ambition has been to become a wife and mother and to enjoy my family. After some discussion and soul searching, we outlined some directions.

First, we believe that adversity could challenge each member of our family and bring out the best in each of us. Applying the synergistic principle, it is possible for the family unit to exceed the combined results of each member. In essence, the whole could exceed the sum of the parts.

Although quite academic at the time, we had read in sacred and secular literature that suffering can bring strength of character. I'm not sure we believed it or were willing to pay that price for enhancing our character. It sounded like claiming a moral victory after losing a close game.

Second, we decided to redouble our emphasis on love being the theme of our family unity, not the Hollywood style but the early Christian version, surpassing the *filial* love of family members to the *agape* love of God for his children. (More about this in chapter 5.)

Third, we adopted a trite but true slogan that "the family that plays and prays together stays together." Physical separation was not a threat. But we were concerned about emotional separation. We wanted more than to avoid fragmentation. We wanted cohesive unity. In the early sixties the nation was beginning to see the breakdown of family units. Maybe as we faced adversity we would develop stronger family ties. It was worth dreaming about and giving it a try.

Fourth, we decided to practice the economic principle of division of labor. Every family member needed to bail water if we were to stay afloat. Everyone needed to hoist a sail if we were to get to our destination. Girls probably fit into such a crew more easily than boys. (Bob fit into the crew since he had grown up doing housework in his home beginning at age ten. During the 1930s he hired out in the neighborhood as a houseboy.) Yard work, housework, errands, meal preparation, laundry were all divided among the four of us. They honored me as the skipper of our crew. This was not the first time that fantasizing guided me through a storm.

Fifth, we decided to use our financial resources for family enjoyment rather than long-term economic security. This was a hard one for Bob to swallow. It got stuck in the throat of his pocket-book! His studies at the School of Business at Kansas University did not point his thinking in that direction. My woman's intuition had strong vibrations about this. I tried to make the point that what good would it do for us to accumulate quantities of money for retirement if we could not enjoy it?

Sixth, we would need to depend upon the family of God to help us through the rough seas. Sometimes I think the psychological professions have done us a disfavor in framing dependency as a bad scene. Maybe the Puritan ethic of the self-made person and rugged individualism made its contribution also. But it completely ignores the contribution to be made by society to the individual. The Wieuca Road Baptist Church family has been a source of strength beyond measure. Without their total support these twenty-some years, our rough seas would have taken on hurricane force.

An independent spirit was born and bred into me as a girl in the Ozark region of Missouri: the show-me state. But when I get into deep water and seem to be going down for the third time, that is no time to refuse the life raft thrown by a caring friend—any port in a storm, any rope for a struggling mate thrown overboard. God grant that in some way I can be a lifesaver for someone else.

General prescription for accepting one's condition: this anonymous poem was found in a Southern home following the Civil War.

Prayer

I asked God for strength that I might achieve,
I was made weak, that I might learn humbly to obey.
I asked for health, that I might do greater things,
I was given infirmity that I might do better things.
I asked for riches, that I might be happy.
I was given poverty, that I might be wise.
I asked for power, that I might have the praise of men,
I was given weakness, that I might feel the need of God.
I asked for all things, that I might enjoy life,
I was given life, that I might enjoy all things.
I got nothing that I asked for—
but everything I had hoped for.
Almost despite myself,
my unspoken prayers were answered.
I am among all men,
most richly
blessed.

—By an Unknown Confederate Soldier

SECTION TWO

Coping Is More Than Trying

5
Coping Within the Family

The previous section (chapters 1-4) was necessary to set the story into perspective. If you are a long-term patient, a family member, or friend, you probably needed some way to identify.

Now comes the practical section—specifically how to cope with limitations. These are not intended to be a "How to do it" series. Rather, you may profit from our trial-and-error experience. Maybe you can use a suggestion or two. Surely, you can improve and modify to suit your situation.

Coping with an Achieving Mate

My lack of physical achievement would be less traumatic if I did not compare it with Bob's ability to get things done. He can clear the dinner table, load the dishwasher, clear the counters, and be through in fifteen minutes. (Maybe a cracked dish now and then and a streaky chrome plate, but it suffices.) It takes me upwards to an hour. He helps to direct a nationwide mission agency and keeps five or six other irons in the fire. And I seem just to do well to keep body and soul together.

Earlier posed questions keep passing through my thoughts: What worth do I have in the world when I accomplish so little? Will I eventually become totally helpless and dependent? Why doesn't God heal me so I can use my energies to help others? (You see, no matter how well you handle these basic questions, they still must be reanswered.)

Life at times seems too routine and bland. When this reality is complicated by medical malfunctions, it is easy to get the blahs. Bob is an author, traveler, sportsman, church leader, and minister to the needs of many persons. And what do I do? The same old sixes and sevens.

I have been fearful that I would embarrass him at business conferences, conventions, wedding receptions, and traveling. All of his assurances that I am not a negative input into his public life have not completely solved the frustration. Had I never functioned normally, fewer questions would come to mind.

It was not until I realized that I brought a positive note to Bob's achievement that I found relief. He had been assuring me of this, but I failed to see this benefit.

● He receives unreserved support of my entire personality. He knows that he is undergirded by my prayers daily, often hourly. His successes and failures are internalized with me. Again, we are two persons become one.

● His achievements receive greater appreciation from his peers and public because of my struggle. It is not pity but their respect for the both of us. Perhaps our Sunday School class members express it best. After weeks of learning with Bob teaching, someone will say, "Don't think that Bob is the only teacher in our classroom. Opha's presence and living example is a learning experience for us also."

● I share in his life as much as possible. Since the girls are grown and out of the house, traveling with him on some of his business trips becomes possible. Often when traveling about the country, we contact some home missionaries in the area of our business destination. We invite them for dinner and an opportunity to share/see their work. It becomes a double blessing and inspiration for both couples.

● Visits to friends in the hospitals are made more meaningful when they know that both of us made time to come.

● In his writings, I serve as the speller, editor, and typist. This has been exceptionally productive therapy. It has kept my fingers somewhat dexterous while feeling useful in religious journalism. During these years, I have typed manuscripts for six books and more than two hundred articles. It has been a chore at times and frustrating at others. For an experienced typist to be reduced to hunt and peck has tried my patience and pushed several deadlines to the limit.

● Attending sporting events and musical productions are physically difficult but worth the planning and effort involved because it includes me in his life. It takes some planning to get seats ahead of time on the aisle, without steps, and near the rest room. This often means arriving very early to get a close parking spot. Likewise, it requires leaving before the end of the event to avoid the crowds.

● Choosing a common hobby in 1980 was wise. In getting ready for retirement within the next seven years, we chose model railroading. I can help plan and purchase as well as create the scenery. We have spent some choice hours in the basement just getting this hobby set up. No telling how many hours of creative pleasure we will enjoy together with our children, grandchildren, other family, and friends. It is surprising how many people have an interest in trains.

● Greatest of all must be our common spiritual interests. When life becomes hectic, and we are scratched deep enough, we will make decisions on spiritual foundations. This solves many problems for us with which other couples must struggle. Do we go to church today? Should we tithe our income? Do we use alcoholic beverages? Do we get caught up in materialism? Do we share and share alike in Bob's earned income? Basically, do we treat each other like we want to be treated?

Coping As a Mother of Growing Daughters

You may recall one of our goals was to raise a well-rounded family. Was MS going to limit that? Would it embitter the girls against marriage?

I did not want to be an embarrassment to the girls especially in front of their peers. It meant laying plans so I would not have to walk with the Brownie troop on the nature hunt. It caused me to have an excuse not to make the long trek to the camp-fire services at church camp. We always arrived at school programs early so I could be seated without notice.

Later, we would use the wheelchair to get to our destination but fold and store it out of view. Open house for PTA was a challenge; parents must move from room to room. When the girls went away to college, they had matured enough to be proud of whatever effort was made to support them. They made me be their "champion," so there was no need to disguise my handicap.

An inborn motherly instinct was threatened by the possibility of not being able to physically assist them as they grew. The demands of children who needed everything from cookies to fresh clothing, teenagers who needed overnight house parties to top-coats shortened or lengthened, young ladies who needed sex education to driver education, college students who needed most everything.

There were wedding plans that excluded mothers formally being seated, receptions that were informal to avoid long periods of standing, declining the walk down the Grand Canyon, using the excuse that the sun was too hot that day.

Memory recalls only one occasion when the girls acted unresponsively. Each had invited a friend to join them on a family vacation to Canada. We were at Banff, and their enthusiasm for horseback riding had caused them to be thoughtless of my situation. (Bob called it rude!) He called our girls aside and gave them a few well-chosen words. No one ever confessed what he said, but the girls had tears in their eyes. A part of my security is that Bob will not tolerate anyone taking unfair advantage of me.

The girls seemed able to accept my limitations in direct proportion to our acceptance of it. This was strong motivation to keep my attitudes positive. We told them more about the prognosis as they were able to understand it mentally and absorb it psychologically.

Some of my better efforts to cope were:

● Teaching the girls about homemaking techniques beginning about their eighth year. I probably spent as much time trying to devise ways to make it fun as I did in actually instructing them. Bob assigned the tasks about the yard. (Nancy detests cleaning up shrubbery prunings to this day! But Daddy never said they were going to enjoy all yard work.)

• While most mothers were spending time in social events or working outside the home, I had the time to work with our girls in the home. They enjoyed learning to sew clothing they could actually wear and to prepare food that was tasty.

• Some of my friends said they have problems in overmothering their children. No real problem for me. During their years of puberty, I just mentioned to Bob it was his time to go to bat for our team. (An old Chinese proverb must have said, "When in doubt, delegate!") And it worked. He said for years he wondered when the father was supposed to take the lead in child development. It makes sense. My mother-hen instinct might have kept the chicks in the nest until they were married; Bob always encouraged them to get out and fly on their own, even if it meant a temporarily bruised body or a banged-up ego.

• Since I could not always go shopping with the girls, we discovered a better idea for them and me. Naturally, they wanted to have name-brand clothing like their friends and a new wardrobe every change of season. Their friends enjoyed such stylish amenities. But their friends' fathers were not earning ministers' salaries. What to do? We gave each girl a clothing credit allowance for the next twelve months. They could spend it for anything they wanted at any time they wanted. If they had any left over at year's end, it could apply to next year's allowance. What happened? They learned budget stretching by shopping the sales. "Villager" labels did not look as attractive as before. Combinations of mix and match provided variety without sameness. Most of all they learned financial responsibility. In the process, I learned to enjoy being carefree about it all.

• "Never on Friday" was the answer to several family dilemmas and my answer to being socially active with the girls. Bob was involved in some form of church activity about four nights a week at Wieuca Road Church. This did not leave him much time to be with the girls. It left me more time than I had strength and energy. We agreed to save Friday night for family and allow the girls to decide where we ate, what we would do, and if they wanted some of their friends to join us. A bonanza! They looked forward to their father's involvement. It provided me relief for the active occasion. The girls took pride in having a night reserved for their pleasure. "Never on Friday" lasted through junior high. After that they had other plans, naturally.

● Grandmothertime is a time of delayed compensation. How sweet it is to see mature concepts of mothering blooming in our daughters. Apparently the cycle will begin all over again as our granddaughter comes to realize that "something is different with Grandmother's walk."

● In all relationships with the girls I tried to help them see that everyone is handicapped in some way. What was theirs? How were they going to handle it? How could they help others adjust to the barriers of a handicap?

● Perhaps the most taxing attempt to cope was the planning of Nancy's second wedding. It was ten years after her first, and I felt many times weakened. But what was I to do? Sit back passively and refuse to give support? Not on your life. Besides, Nancy needed my support more the second time around.

Where there is a will, there is a way. This was an opportunity to demonstrate our love and acceptance of her husband to be. They had dated steadily for several years. We wanted her to enjoy the fulfillment of a happy married life as Linda had. The only thing we knew to do to help was to pray. But how do you pray and for what? As usual, it came down to asking that God's will could be done in her life.

One evening she telephoned, chatting about mother-daughter concerns. For the first time in years she said she wanted both parents on the line. Out of the blue she surprised us with "Joe and I want to get married. What do you think about a patio wedding in our backyard on Father's Day?" We responded enthusiastically, for it was her decision for her life. It's a good thing we did, for she replied, "I forgot to tell you that Joe is on the other line!"

● Maybe the best encouragement to keep on keeping on was overhearing the girls telling each other that "Our mom is the best sport we know. She is our champion."

Coping as a Relative Separated by Miles

The first church we served was in Saint Joseph, Missouri, only forty miles from Kansas City. But our next move to Greenville, South Carolina, brought a separation from both families of 900 miles. The Binghams and the Stumps are close-knit families, but knitting can become loose at that distance. Was I to be the disabled family member seldom heard from and less likely seen?

● The annual visit back home became an event. That was made easier as my folks always gave us a half of beef to take home. It meant driving that distance without an overnight to keep the meat frozen. We conjured all kinds of fun games in which all participated . . . and fiercely competed. Even though Bob usually drove most of the distance, he could throw the yatzee dice into a large box, get a reading on the dice from someone and make his selection.

● We encouraged the families in Missouri to plan events the girls would enjoy. They gladly cooperated and relieved me from considerable exertion while at our destination. Cousins and neighboring friends made easy playmates. And who needs much planned entertainment on a farm?

Bob has always encouraged me to utilize the telephone. What woman doesn't? But he included long distance calls. What a substitute for ambulation! A weekly call to parents and less frequently to siblings narrowed the distance. College days raised the cost, but we loved it. Linda epitomized the concept when calling to announce the arrival of the first grandchild. Her opening words were, "Beth Lacy calling collect to announce her arrival. Will you accept the charges?" Well trained, that girl!

Then there were short one-minute calls after 5:00 PM and on weekends. I could call friends all over the country and begin with,

"Hi, this is Opha. Just have sixty seconds to say I'm thinking about you and wish we could be with you in person. But I guess my telephone call and spirit will have to suffice." We share a bit of news and call it off, all of the intense personal exchange for thirty-five cents a minute. Maybe the zenith of that type of interfacing came last Christmas when we called our friends in Belfast, Ireland. It took a little longer: one minute for him to get over the shock, another minute to summon his wife, and then a brief, but meaningful exchange.

● While my handwriting is sporadic, my electric typewriter is dependable. Letters and cards do not have to be lengthy to be appreciated. Having a newsy note in the mailbox was a pleasure long before the Pony Express. When my mother was in a nursing home, it was all the more important that I keep in close touch with her. Physical separation was hard on me as well as her. It always helped my spirit to cheer hers.

Bob chides me that I may overdo the sending of notes: thank you, birthday, get well, friendship notes, and notes for any and all occasions. But I need that outlet. And it extends my personality and witness around the country. Sometimes I may get carried away . . . like thanking a person for writing me a lengthy thank-you note for something I had done for them. That could have gone forever if I had not run out of stamps about that time.

● The families' morale needs to be assured that all is well in Atlanta. A part of my fulfillment in life is to be an encouragement to others. I hear them saying, "If Opha can keep going and smiling, surely I can too."

● Reunions for families that stretch from Denver, Colorado, to Myrtle Beach, South Carolina, are not easy to pull off. But they are worth the effort. The cross fertilization of the cousins by the dozens is a thing to behold. It enables me to visit everyone with one trip. And who doesn't want a vacation on the beach or in the Rockies?

● Don't forget that distance separating relatives is a mixed blessing. Too much proximity too often takes the excitement from the encounter. Such homespun philosophy has helped me to accept other limitations put upon me.

• In all fairness, it should be mentioned my coping was made possible by family members learning how to cope with me. Most tough roads are "two-way streets." Unless you have limped in my shoes, you will never know what a difference it can make when you know that your family supports you. Day in and day out— which runs into year in and year out.

Let me briefly tell you. (Since Bob is helping to write this account, I feel he will represent himself well throughout the book, and I'll major on other members of our family.)

Linda is an absentee daughter in geography only. A couple of notes a week (with plenty of snapshots) and usually a telephone call on the weekends keep my spirit up. Michael is our first son, and he came along by marrying Linda. His thoughtfulness to Linda and Beth (the birth of whom gave me the blessed disease of "grandmotheritis") is matched by his desire to please me. Not once have I spent any energy wondering if that family had their act together.

Nancy has lived in Atlanta except for a short span after her first marriage. While she and I both need independence, we also know that we need each other. How strange of God to create his children with seemingly opposite emotional needs. In spite of Nancy's struggle to find a meaningful existence on a road that always seemed uphill, she finds time to share her love and appreciation to me. And gratefully, she has given us a second son Joe by marriage just last summer.

My sister and brother have been so concerned and have shown it, even when separated by nearly a thousand miles. Eunice has nursed me through several recuperations. Hubert annually provides us with a side of Western-aged prime beef. What a practical way to be thoughtful! Even more important, they both support me in their prayers to our Heavenly Father. Bob's family has taken me into their "clan": before MS, because it is their nature to include others inside the family circle; after MS, in recognition of the effort it takes to want to keep up with the family.

When I notice how many families tend to shun the handicapped member, it gives me strength and endurance to receive their regular support.

Contributions to Our Family and the Family of God

Since physical contribution is limited, perhaps I can make my input spiritually. In spite of Bob's being an ordained minister, he publically claims that I am the spiritual leader of our family. (All of that praise without a woman's lib campaign!) I am not sure he is right, but it does motivate me to exert some leadership at that point.

It seems I have gained spiritual strength through physical weakness. Perhaps it forced me to practice the primacy of the spirit, a doctrine we often preach but seldom practice. I have tried to recall some evidence to support Bob's claim. Here are some examples:

● Daily Devotions.—Continue to encourage daily devotions, even though hectic time schedules make it difficult. Everyone seems to be busy these days. But too busy to commune with God and read his Word is too busy, indeed.

● Friends.—My friends often contact me for counsel: maybe because I am available at home, maybe because I am willing, maybe because I have something to give. A country philosopher phrased it, "You can't give what you don't have any more than you can come back from where you ain't been." No question that I have been there.

● Church.—While holding no official position, I seem to have spiritual elevation in the hearts of the members. One of the blessings in being able to put down roots over a twenty-year period is that people have an opportunity to size you up and put their confidence in you. Some people achieve and merit such trust in a few months. Some of us take longer. But a confidence slowly gained is seldom quickly lost. Men and women have found a listening ear.

• Ministry.—I minister by visiting the sick, aged, and home-bound, calling lonely people on the telephone, inviting childless couples into our home on holidays, baking and cooking for families in sickness and sorrow—the time is worth the struggle.

• Prayers.—I have worked in a mission church since 1982. What a lift the concerned prayers of the righteous have been to me. By the same token, what a joy to hold others up in prayer to our Heavenly Father.

• The Word of God.—Hopefully, you will find strength and encouragement in these favorite passages of Scripture:

Psalm 23	John 3:16
Matthew 5:16	Matthew 6:33-34
Matthew 7:7-8	John 14:27
Romans 5:1-5	2 Corinthians 12:9
Romans 8:28	James 1:22

• Dependence on God.—Becoming dependent upon God for life and strength, I can be free to be independent in matters of the spirit.

• Public Worship.—Regular public worship restores the soul, and intercessory prayer keeps open a close relationship with God through Christ.

General Prescription for Coping Within the Family of God: recognize that a long-term illness may be the agent that will bring your "family" closer together rather than possible estrangement.

6
Coping with Travel

Travel has always been in Bob's blood, and I must admit it is contagious. For a south Missouri girl who seldom traveled beyond a two hundred mile radius, you can imagine the potential excitement.

The girls' first few years had been low-traveling years due to their ages, Mother Bingham's declining illness, and our moderate income. With the move to Atlanta we were ready to go. All aboard! But before we could get out of the station, we heard "MULTIPLE SCLEROSIS." Would it put the brakes to the train? Would I have the energy? The desire? Could we afford it?

We concluded that our family life could be celebrated with a family trip each year. As mentioned earlier, Bob's church engagements usually consumed four nights a week. We needed the long, quality-time vacation. Trips could be arranged to fit my pace. If we did not have the money, we could borrow it. (On the last night of one such trip we figured how much our family saved by refraining from alcoholic drinks and smoking for one year. Believe it or not, these savings financed one half of that year's trip.)

Then in 1962, we were planning a trip to some of the great national parks of the West. Bob did not see how we could finance it and still make our modest mutual fund investment. It was here I threw out the caution flag. Were our priorities going to be long-term investments for financial resources? Or short-term investments for human resources? Bob made a *U* turn, and we began to plan for a trip that possibly might be our last. (Actually, Linda and Bob were the planners. They wrote for maps and pamphlets and studied them for months to get the best trip for the money.) We all continued to receive returns on our travel investments.

I was always ready to go. It was never a question of should I go. But when and where could we go next? Ready and willing but not always able. No need to bore you with a travelogue.

This is not to imply that traveling does not bring its own inconveniences. Service stations are not always readily available according to my bladder needs nor medical care around the corner. Lodging accommodations are not customarily designed to be barrier free. Although each year brings progress. Physical strength may not continue to roll on, even though the miles do. Adrenaline has a problem remaining high for several weeks at a time. My eyes are bigger than my stomach, and my heart is stronger than my legs.

Only once did we have a close call with death while traveling. We were visiting missionaries through southern New York state in beautiful, rural country. Fortunately, we had arrived in Niagara Falls, Ontario, for the weekend. Before getting my first view of the Falls, a stomach pain turned into a visit to the emergency room. In three hours they had me on the operating table and extracted an infarcted half of my lower intestine which had become twisted somehow. The intestine was gangrenous and ready to burst. Thank God for skilled Canadian doctors, nurses, surgeons, and the total hospital team!

What an opportunity to witness to our faith! Bob says I was hardly out of the recovery room before telling anyone who would listen how great our God is. In Bob's free time he could visit the patients on the floor. The hospitality director made him unofficial chaplain of the third floor. I shared from my abundance of floral arrangements, giving to those patients who had few or none.

What a homecoming to fly back to Atlanta (two weeks following surgery). We could truly thank God for his protection through trials, tribulations, and travel.

Hints for Overcoming Barriers

Like many a valued experience, there are two special times: the beginning and the end. That includes becoming a boat owner, having our grandchildren visit, and traveling. The excitement to return home almost equates the joy of going. There seems to be something emotionally wholesome about that. Life back at the ranch must be pretty good after all. Here are some helps with coping along the way.

● *Planning.*—No matter what anyone tells you, take the time (and pleasure) for making specific, detailed itineraries. The come-what-may approach may provide creative thrills for the excitement seekers. But it is no bargain for the handicapped traveler. Research the motels that have barrier-free accommodations. Plan your trip based on the maximum miles you can travel a day. Write several motels and ask for brochures showing their property and a statement related to barrier-free accommodations. Note in AAA travel books and motel chain catalogs which motels are equipped for handicapped persons. (Usually designed with the handicapped symbol following the telephone listing.)

Write the Department of Transportation and/or the Department of Tourism in each state/city/country you wish to visit. Ask for information and materials. Also, visit your travel agent and pick up free brochures. Look for bargains for any reason at any time. You will be surprised at the savings you can effect in off-season travel. Write the National Park Service, US Department of the Interior, Washington, DC, for a copy of *Access to National Parks, A Guide for Handicapped Visitors.* This is an excellent book moderately priced.

A visit to your local public library should round out your research.

● *Group Travel.*—This kind of travel is a mixed blessing. By some selective choices of traveling companions you can make it a predictably happy experience. Idiosyncrasies tend to multiply in number and intensity when we travel. By taking an overnight

"trial run" with others, you can usually get an idea of your compatibility. I have difficulty if those traveling with me do not understand my handicap. Large tour groups while less expensive are out
of the question. There are too many people, too many scheduled
stops, too many places to see too often—just too much. I'd rather
go less often.

Four to a group is often ideal, especially if you wish to rent a
car. Only walking is cheaper. (Honeymooners may want two-
alone privacy, but they will get over that.) The friends that have
traveled with us have added many positive dimensions to our trips.
We plan the trips together and therefore minimize the frustration
of the disappointing surprises not quite measuring up to our
dreams.

● *Helping Hands.*—People are usually ready and willing to help
the handicapped person. When our wheelchair approaches a
crowd, it is like the dividing of the Red Sea. Without suggestion,
a self-appointed "Moses" appears to direct the traffic. Airport and
hotel personnel regularly offer assistance. Some unusual experiences are worth mentioning. At the winter palace in Leningrad we
were faced with a marble staircase with about seventy steps and
no elevator. While we were pondering whether to attempt to
navigate the staircase, two Russian men strolled by. In jovial sign
language they promptly picked up my chair and smoothly carried
me to the top.

During the time in Niagara Falls we were stranded for two
weeks because of emergency surgery. Bob visited the nearest Baptist church to worship on Sunday; they offered him a bedroom,
meals, and the use of an auto. Later, a motel owner made a special
phone available to him and drove us to the Buffalo airport for our
flight home.

● *Train Travel.*—When you have the time and want to see the
countryside, it is the best way to go. The new Amtrak equipment
has special compartments for sleeping, each completely equipped
for the handicapped. Because the equipment is lightweight, it
therefore tends to shake a bit on the rails. If your muscles and

bladder can adjust, you should have a pleasant experience. Notify your local station agent twenty-four hours in advance. He will arrange complete boarding details for you. The dining or car attendant will bring your hot meals or snacks to your compartment. The cost for these specialized compartments are no more than regular bedroom accommodations. Write to "Access Amtrak" for a guide to Amtrak services available for elderly and handicapped travelers from your local Amtrak agent.

• *Airplanes.*—These make travel easiest: quick, safe, convenient, demanding less energy. Their personnel are especially trained to look after your special needs. Twenty-four hour advance notice is helpful, but they respond to instant needs. Most major lines provide identical services although some personnel are more accommodating.

Make your reservations early. This may save you money from a fare increase and assure your choice seat request near the rest room and on the aisle, if necessary. If you travel tourist class, request the first row behind the bulkhead. Advise them of any special dietary needs. When checking in at the ticket counter, advise the agent of your specific handicap and ask for any needed help. Check through all luggage to your destination. Make sure each article is properly tagged with your name, address, and telephone number.

Arrive one hour before flight time. This helps their personnel meet your needs, not to mention relieving your anxiety level. Beginning with the skycaps at the curb, the ticket agents, the special agents, the gate agents, and the flight attendants; each can be a vital link in making your flight a pleasant one.

Upon arriving at the departure gate, tell the agent if you will need a carryon chair. Or if you are taking your own wheelchair, it should be tagged and ready for baggage. Also if you will need help at your destination, mention any special needs that might be overlooked. Since the rest room is usually forward near the first-class seats, inquire of the possibility of using first-class facilities. Be ready for an early boarding call which will allow you time to be seated before the rush of regular passengers. The flight attendants are free at the early boarding time to give you extra assistance.

Early into your flight remind the flight attendant if you will need any extra assistance and if you wish your wheelchair brought to the cabin door. The latter will save you problems. You do not have to wait for a skycap to bring an airport chair and then pick your chair up at the baggage claim counter.

• *Auto Travel.*—This kind is most frequently used by us. Five hundred miles or a ten-hour day of travel is possible at 55 miles per hour. We plan a rest room stop every two hours to eliminate the trauma of an "accident." As a by-product, the regular stop helps circulation and muscle tone. Lunch is picked up at a fast-food place.

We have found these extra helps beneficial. A wheelchair carrier mounted to the back bumper saves space and problems in lifting the chair out of the trunk. A hanging strap securely mounted over your door makes getting in and out of the car much easier. A portable, car pottie can be purchased or personally created to give immediate urinary relief if bladder control is questionable.

Auto travel can become tiring if only from boredom. Overcome this by planning special topics of conversation for which you seldom have time to discuss in your daily routine. We usually discuss financial matters with which we wives need help: current conditions and particularly conditions in the event of a spouse's death. We finally reduced these matters to writing, so I can recall them more accurately. There is no use in having a needless additional handicap during the bereavement time.

Another way to be a good steward of long days of travel is to discuss some ticklish matters where you have lack of agreement. So often these matters require plenty of uninterrupted time—time to talk it through to completion. These ways of redeeming the time have been so much more productive than napping, knitting, or doing nothing.

• *Accommodations.*—These are improving every year. New units are required by government regulations to have some barrier-free accommodations available. Smaller facilities will usually plan parking just outside your room door. By requesting a first-floor room when making motel reservations, you eliminate climbing steps or going through a lobby to an elevator and down a long corridor. You are likely to need something left in the car, and the proximity of the auto is important.

If you are flying, the larger hotels will have more services and often larger accommodations. If in doubt, check if the hotel has an 800 telephone number to call free. If they do not, make an evening rate long-distance call to assure your hotel stay will be a pleasant one.

If you have weak legs, beware of the airport van to the hotel. The first step into the van is almost a moon leap. I seldom can make it unless we purposely have taken a hard piece of luggage on which I can stand, using this as my first step. Even then Bob often must bend and guide my legs to the floor of the van. Do not expect the van to be equipped with a portable, steel step. Taxis may refuse to take you to a nearby hotel (because of the small fare after waiting so long in line). However, if you will tell the taxi starter of your problem in getting into a van, he will secure a taxi for you. A more than average tip will relieve his pain.

Room service is not designed for the rich only. For a reasonable service charge you can have food brought to your room. This may help you to conserve your energy for more enjoyable vacation or business purposes.

● *Medicines.*—Medicines need to be easily available and are a must when you are away from home. Pack all your regular medicine and any other that you might need for an emergency. Remember to carry an extra pair of eyeglasses if needed and extra prescriptions for extended trips. Have your physician's telephone number handy.

● *Family Travel.*—How many times we have heard other families bemoan their family auto trips: too much noise, too many people, too much activity, too frequent stops for cola and candy. Too bad for the trip! The most-voiced complaint was that the children could not get along in the car. Or they did not enjoy the same experiences as the parents.

We must have lucked into the solution, at least for parents with two daughters. Both of the girls were encouraged to invite a friend of their choosing to go on the trip. (Their parents paid for food and lodging.) The girls had "their own" room with two double beds sleeping the four. They traveled together in the back seat. We could all eat together or separately. Our girls helped determine the itinerary. Every person in the car had a special chore to make the trip more enjoyable.

● *Miscellaneous.*—If your mobility is limited, take along extra reading material, crafts, games, puzzles, pencil, and paper. Who knows, you may be writing a book! Seriously, there will always be times that your limitations will cause you to wait until others return. Be prepared. Whip out those items and enjoy those hours.

Use the wheelchair as a baggage carrier. When Bob pushes the chair and we cannot locate a bellhop or skycap, we improvise. We stack both pieces of luggage on my knees, place the two hanging bags over the top of the luggage, and amble on to the room self-contained. Sometimes I barely see over the top, but Bob is the driver. We probably have avoided collisions because people have avoided us. Some may have "died"—laughing to death! The chair's back pouch serves to hold the mini umbrella with the strap double wrapped around the push handles. My lap is often covered with handbag, knitting bag, and the like.

Travel need not be only to faraway places with strange-sounding names. Wedding anniversaries have been celebrated in an Atlanta hotel. Parts of this manuscript have been written in the mountains of North Carolina and the beaches of South Carolina.

General prescription for travel: it is a three-for-one bargain. It enables you to vacate your all-too-common environment—with your mind as you plan the trip, with your body as you experience the trip, with your soul as you relive the trip and store memories.

7
Coping with Myself

Pogo was right: we have met the enemy, and he is us. Perhaps my greatest barrier is myself. It is one thing to joust with a real adversary. It is another thing to tilt with the windmills. But it is perhaps most fearsome to wrestle on the battleground with yourself. It is easy to shift the blame or responsibility to others, but we have no easy outlet when the struggle lies within.

Rationalizing away the reality of our inner problems never solves them. We must face them, objectify them, and persevere to overcome them. No one ever told me it would be a cakewalk. Yet no one ever said that living with severe limitations for more than twenty years would be so demanding.

Discipline, determination, and divine direction have been constant companions in my pilgrimage. Early on I promised myself to try to keep my personality crystal clear to reflect the basic joy, happiness, and peace the Christian needs to express. (Little did I know that often someone or something would rain on my parade!)

Loneliness acts like a cancer to all handicaps. How odd that someone might choose to withdraw from society when the handicap appears to be roadblock size. Voluntary withdrawal seems as counterproductive as voluntary cancer, but let's face it. When your general muscular activity is limited throughout your body, you will have temptations to withdraw. Your husband, family, and friends all seem to enjoy many stimulating activities, and there you sit at home. Boredom bores in if you give it a soft spot.

God blessed me with a caring family. Each member makes a contribution to my pilgrimage. Seldom do they load me up with their baggage. Regularly do they push me along with expressed appreciation. Such positive expressions make me more determined to make a Christian home worthy of the name. Boredom makes its exit when we look for avenues to serve others.

One simple outlet has been to invite some lady friends to go to lunch with me. They provide the transportation, and I provide the lunch, or we "Dutch" it. A large shopping center is within a mile of our home, and it provides proximity, shopping, fellowship, and lunch. Shopping is difficult for me. It takes so much energy, and crowds clutter up my traffic pattern in the stores. I miss browsing and comparing prices. Bob never has understood why we ladies like to "shop." He is a typical male shopper: know what item you want, find it in the store, and buy it. That's why I need my friends with whom to shop. But I find it hard to ask them to give up a couple of hours in the middle of the day. Perhaps my own reticence is self-defeating.

Every normal human needs some degree of fulfillment. Handicapped people tend to feel shortchanged at this point. When the girls left the "nest" several years ago, I wanted to enter the ranks of the employed again. Or maybe do more volunteer work. But the road signs on that trip kept saying, "Too fatigued," "Irregular hours," "Unpredictability," "Inflexibility."

The pay was not a major consideration. I wanted to convince myself I still had marketable skills; I could make a contribution to society. The adult contacts would be stimulating. The challenge would drive me to meet the demands operating in the real world.

But roadblocks were everywhere. Which days would I have enough mobility to get to the work place? If I got there, would my secretarial hands function as desired and required? If fatigue set in, where could I rest? Would a regular hourly job make demands I could predictably meet? Would the job routine prevent me from traveling with Bob when the opportunity came? For one reason or another, I never sought outside employment. Regular volunteer work might have been more flexible and less demanding. Yet my level of acceptable performance made its own demands.

Do you remember the classic television commercial of the early sixties when the little daughter responds, "Mother, I'd rather do it myself"? A case for the need of personal achievement. My handicap underscored the need to achieve. Even if it meant just being able to dress myself, shut the car door, shuffle a deck of cards, or sweep the patio. Not to mention preparing tasty meals, keeping the house attractive, and doing the family laundry. Sounds like I am not handicapped, doesn't it? You must understand that it takes me many times longer to complete a simple task that only took a few minutes to achieve in my healthier years.

Bob always wants to help. But the temptation to overhelp is a fine line. In his desire to serve me he takes away my desire to do it myself, no matter how cumbersome and lengthy the chore may seem. By the same token he often overprotects me, and I want to shout, "I'm a big girl and can take care of myself." Maybe husbands take on the mothering aspect of companionship when the mother is incapacitated. And if Bob has temptations at this point, you can be assured that less understanding friends are always wanting to help me do things that "I'd rather do myself."

Another recurring question is, "Why can't I have the strength to help others the way I want to?" My life-style since a child has been to offer help whenever I see a need. I still see needs all about me, but I simply cannot meet them. When the able so often are not willing, why can't the willing be able?

It seems we often look for logical answers to satisfy our minds. We are confused by such dilemmas as above; we are forced to search for answers that transcend our mental processes. Bob's search for the answer to why bad things happen to good people is that God turns our weaknesses into strength. He keeps telling me that my witness to a needy world is greatly magnified by my obvious weakness. I hear him. It makes sense. I think I understand. But the next time my physical limitations keep me from helping someone . . . I still wonder!

It is a good thing I have the gift of patience. God knows I need it. How many times in my pre-MS days did the common expression pass through my lips, "Don't we take so many things for granted?" Little did I know how much! My dressing habits were typically feminine. (Bob says that means SLOW.) But both of us have learned what slow dressing is now. Without any pretense of sophisticated makeup procedures, it takes me about sixty minutes to put on my clothing, providing I have already decided what to wear.

Cooking and baking came second nature. My mother baked bread every day of every year until my father died. What is a meal without fresh-baked bread? Working with yeast dough is still enjoyable, if not easy. My lack of feeling in the fingers frustrates me day in and day out. Peeling, slicing, lifting, sifting—all the proportions for cooking makes it hard to predict the recipe's outcome.

And dropping things. If I could just hold on to the things I finally get picked up. Once dropped, it can be a major project to retrieve. Broken glass presents a unique problem. The struggle in the everyday taken-for-granted, simple routines of life leaped before me. Realizing my sense of touch was modulating or disappearing completely, holding on to small items became an unsought challenge. Dropping the dental floss from my fingers and retrieving it too many times caused small punctures in my spirit. Necessity for constant flexibility and creativity surfaced. This is yet another of the countless simple routines taken for granted.

How could the needed patience and personal know-how be found? A childhood remedy reworded to my personal needs has been a constant reminder. One that bends in many usable directions: "If at first you don't succeed, keep on trying 'til you do!"

Lack of balance goes with MS. And lack of balance brings all kinds of unexpected reactions. The simplest might be the embarrassment of people thinking you are inebriated. Others vary in complications from needing constant support to falling and breaking a hip.

"Mrs. Bingham, what are you doing in a wheelchair?" This question pierced my ears as we were racing through the Atlanta airport. I was so hoping we would see no one we knew. It was twelve years ago, and I rarely used the wheelchair. The exclaimer was Sherida, an airline hostess, a former member of my sixth grade Sunday School class. She thought I had been in an accident. I wished her assessment had been right. When I told her I had MS and she said, "There are times when I wish I could use a wheelchair," a feeling of embarrassment came over me. Which would be controlled first: my pride or MS?

Where do you draw the line between safeguarding physical health and jeopardizing emotional stability? I would go crazy if I did not risk some physical security. While I still drive a car with restrictions, it has posed frustration. What risk to myself? What burden to my family if permanently disabled? (Or was I not already permanently disabled?) What risk to other drivers or pedestrians? The one collision I had was my fault and fortunately injured no one.

The need to be independent is paramount. My friends have more important things to do than to take me for the weekly beauty parlor appointment. (Yet this is a very important event in the week for the average lady. Men, take note.) Beauty parlors are not always easy to get to, get around in, or get out of. No parking spaces, crowded inside configurations, and often some steps to navigate. But I never, never, no never consider the possibility of not going!

What do you do when you fall, and no one is around to help? Indoors? Outdoors? When Bob is out of town? When the phone is out of reach? When you collapse on your driveway and the midsummer sun is sapping what available strength is left? First, you holler "HELP!" The real question is, when no one responds what do you do? By far the most disturbing question is not, will anyone ever come? The real kicker comes after the storm is over, and the clouds have passed on. Then you begin to wonder when and where it will happen again?

One day when clipping the ivy, the sun blazed on me like a pansy in the desert. Feeling faint, the only shade available was under the automobile. Navigating the extra ten yards to the back door was out of the question. I fell to my knees and inched under the car for shade: relief. But how long could this be tolerated? After resting (and gasping) for a few minutes, perhaps I should try to yell for help. Large lungs and strong vocal chords were not God-given to me, but I shouted anyway. In a few minutes the next-door neighbor appeared and asked if I needed help.

Another miracle. She recounted that her house was shut up. The air conditioning was droning through the hot day, and she was watching television. Now you tell me how she heard the weakened call for help without God carrying my voice on extra terrestrial wavelengths.

This scene began the search for an alarm system of some kind. A church friend rigged up a homemade alarm, using a garage-door closer as the basic unit. It set off a buzzer in the contiguous houses. Later, this system was refined by a medical/fire/police alert system that sent a telephone impulse to a twenty-four-hour central answering agency. They, in turn, telephone the proper emergency unit plus telephoning three friends and Bob's office, notifying them of the emergency. The unit has been a blessing to me, Bob, our family, and friends. But the question still comes: am I giving in to living in fear?

The apostle John was right when he declared in his first epistle that fear is a tool of Satan. I determined early on not to give in to fear: more easily said than done. Yet if I had not set my course to be one void of as much fear as possible, I would now be a "basket case." There would be no driving, and that would make me a prisoner in my own home. Multilocked doors would only serve to remind me of the possibility of robbery, rape, or murder. To be afraid when alone at night or overnight would have forced continual companion care. Bob would have to turn his back on his calling to minister to people at anytime of the day or night. The fear of kidnapping or mugging in the shopping centers would deprive me of what little shopping I get to do. President Roosevelt was right when he declared to the nation in shock on December 8, 1941: "We have nothing to fear but fear itself."

Embarrassment has been mentioned before. But a lady has some inherent problems with this emotion. And being disabled compounds the reaction. I want to hide the walker and the wheel-chair. When eating I invariably drop food or keep it on my lips. (It doesn't help a bit to know that other people do the same thing. Especially as we get older.) My right hand becomes so weak at times that I cannot always hold an eating utensil.

Foot dragging is not just a figure of speech. It is a fact for every step taken. The right leg must drag regardless of the desire to lift it. Shoes wear out on the toes. Carpets show where I walk. It takes so long to get anywhere. But so what? What really gets to the emotions are the public displays of inadequacy. Busses or vans are nearly impossible barriers. People want to lift me. But such bodily stress separates the ribs from the rib cage, and that is a three-month recuperative process where even breathing is painful. The only way I can mount steps higher than six inches is for Bob to bend my knee using counteractive pressure and manually lifting my foot. What fun with everyone looking and waiting!

And why have the style designers forgotten the handicapped? The zippers are in the wrong places. Sometimes you cannot oper-ate the zipper, and sometimes you are too late anyway. Most everyone wants to look stylish or at least to avoid the vintage of hospital-gown blue. Styles change so quickly, especially if you shop irregularly and then for only an hour at a time, if you wear a size four shoe and a size seven dress that seem to come only in teenage modish fashions.

Coping with My Ego

The situations above only touch the hem of the garment (no pun intended). They are multiplied and squared many times a year. How do you cope with them? Perhaps each person has to decide by trial and error. Many trials and many errors. For the hand-icapped readers, your family and friends, I blush to share with you some of my coping procedures. Some are more personal than I find comfortable to see in print. But if they help you, I can wade through one more pool of embarrassment.

● Shopping.—Oddly enough, Professor Harold Hill in *The Music Man* gave me encouragement to use the catalogs. Obviously, this was not my introduction to mail-order purchasing. (Every rural household during the thirties recognized the Sears and Montgomery Ward catalogs.) They fall short of the Sak's Fifth Avenue Store at the shopping center, but it simplifies things. No, it doesn't take the place of browsing and people watching, but it is an acceptable option. There are dozens of catalogs on the market.

The catalogs do perform a service for those who seldom can get out to shop. Forget the pseudofashions, the nonstandard sizes, the wrinkled and damaged merchandise, the problems in returning unwanted goods. And of course: computer foul-up. Forget those drags on the fun of shopping. Remember: they do provide a service and be thankful for it.

Another option: find a salesperson, buyer, or manager at your favorite store(s) and acquaint them with your needs. They will be on the lookout for you—and their own needs. In my case they have been willing to check out several garments for Bob to bring for my selection. He returns any that are not useful to my needs which are most of them.

● Fulfillment.—Handicapped persons without close church ties are doubly penalized. Obviously, the greatest support of such a relationship is being a participant in a caring fellowship. Coping is hard enough at best. It must be nigh impossible without it.

An important by-product of active church participation is the opportunity to become engaged in meaningful work of the church (not to be confused with "busy work"). Most committed Baptists have more church activities than they can handle. But it is vitally important for me to be involved in telephoning, record keeping, and functioning committees in addition to regular Sunday and weekday meetings. My church life is the balance wheel of my life outside the home.

• Personal needs.—Planning is the key. Plan each day and each event with a generous amount of flexibility. Anticipate needs, even simple ones. My walker had no pocket for carrying things. Obviously both hands are utilized to move the walker. I sewed a "kangaroo pouch" to tie on the top front. Pockets compartmentalize the inside, holding placed articles securely. Included regularly are tongs, long handle shoehorn, glue, stamps, pens, calendar, note pads, tooth brush and paste, personal hygene items, pencil flash light. (Frequent emptying brings certain surprises.)

Friends are amazed what I can carry in the pouch. It's always fun to take coffee orders and return with two cups of coffee, appropriately prepared as ordered. When I pull the three-quarter filled cups out of the pouch, I enjoy the amazed expression on the guests' faces.

Personal body aids need to be placed in all bathrooms plus the bedroom and basement. Mobile people can get to almost any part of their home in ten seconds. Sometimes it could take me several minutes of laborious struggle just to reach a bottle of hand lotion. No wasted energy if you plan to have aids in several places.

Telephone answering can be programmed frustration. Today's caller expects you to answer by the fifth ring. Chances are I cannot get to the phone by that time. We can't afford an extension in every room, so what do you do? First, tell your friends to let the phone ring at least fifteen times. Advise retail stores to write on the order blank, "Let the phone ring a long time." Devise a code ring with your most frequent caller(s).

Since beginning the manuscript the cordless phones have become more prominent. How nice. The receiver is carried in the pouch and can be answered in a few rings. How delightful to be "normal" in this regard.

• Family help.—Discuss thoroughly with each family member with whom you have frequent association. Help them to understand they assist best only at your request. Or, when it is obvious you cannot function without them. Be specific. Be frank. Be grateful. Be loving.

● Dropping things.—Place a pair of long handled tongs in your pouch. Maybe they are the most used aids I have.

● Portable potties.—When mobility was no problem, I failed to see the profundity of the cliché, "When you gotta go, you gotta go." Now, I claim some pride of authorship in the axiomatic declaration. However, for the immobile impaired the question is also, How far do you have to go to go? Your hospital supply house can show you a variety of manufactured portable potties. But have you added your distinctive touch to their options? Have you disguised one within a piece of custom-made furniture to place at your bedside? If nature calls every three hours, the nighttime calls become walking nightmares without a bedside commode. By daytime, no evidence is apparent in this attractive chair.

Obviously, our basement commode will not win the blue ribbon at the furniture show. Your traveling model for hotel or any tourist use may well be the plastic bedpan you brought home from the last hospital visit. It will pack neatly in your hanging clothes bag. In all of this dainty discussion, don't forget to squirrel away rolls of toilet tissue everywhere.

One who is limited in strength and resources has daily confrontations relating to the best use of available energy. The temptation to give up comes to mind over and over. The lure to stay in bed and be served was stronger before I had so many hospitalizations and was forced to stay in bed. But I'll have to admit that often I am so weary of it all that the bed seems an easy way out. It has been helpful to jot down special lines or verses that tend to cast out the temptation.

General Prescription for Coping with Yourself: if you gotta handicap, you gotta cope. If you gotta cope, you gotta plan ahead. If you gotta plan, you gotta forget perfection!

"The way to a man's heart"—I fed Bob wedding cake at our wedding reception (April 3, 1947, in Kansas City, MO).

Even in their younger days, our daughters supported me emotionally—Linda on the left and Nancy.

Our family posed around the fireplace in 1966—Bob, me, Nancy, and Linda.

On one of our cruises the ships' captain and Bob literally were stabilizing me.

We were admiring Linda shortly before the wedding.

Here we were at our 1981 family reunion in North Carolina. See if you can spot Linda, Nancy, Bob, and me.

"Granny Opha" with Linda, her husband Michael Lacy, and their baby Beth

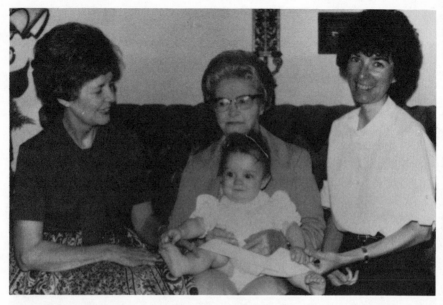

Great grandmother, grandmother, and Linda "sit for the birdie" with baby Beth.

"Duke" Bob and "Duchess" Opha show a book to Beth.

Here I am going up the stairs with the wash (Mark Sandlin Photo).

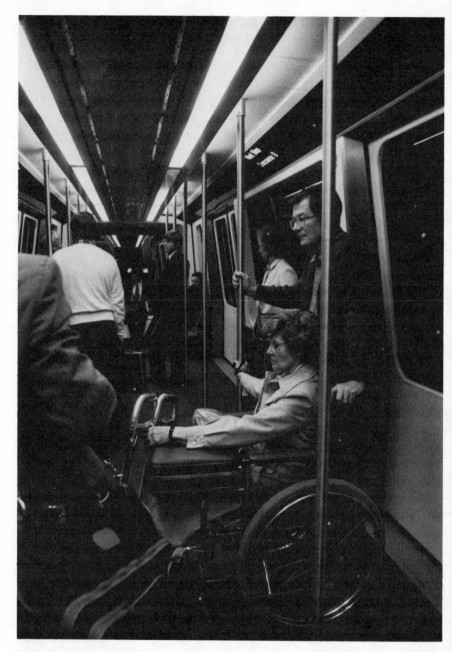

We've never let my "handicap" stop us from traveling. Here we're riding the shuttle at the airport (Mark Sandlin Photo).

Bob and I walk up the hill in the park (Mark Sandlin Photo).

We often stop to talk with store clerks about quality and price. It's fun shopping together (Mark Sandlin Photo).

We, the Duke and Duchess, holding Beth, sit for our 1983 Christmas photo. Linda and her husband Michael Lacy are on the left rear, and Nancy and her husband Joe Dunaway are on the right (Mark Sandlin Photo).

Outside enjoying the sun (Mark Sandlin Photo)

8
Coping with the Unexpected

Nobody promised me a rose garden. But life is filled with roses, if we only take time to stop and smell them. But watch out for the thorns! How unexpected is the sensation of pain the first time a child grabs for a rose.

The books on MS helped to prepare me for the expected. Perhaps they could not anticipate the unexpected. By definition, these come in differing packages for all of us. Most people learn to deal with such crises from a base of strength, but for those with long-term disability we must cope from a base of physical weakness.

Lest I misrepresent my situation, let me write that my general health is excellent . . . outside of MS and its many complications. The annual physical is always encouraging. No blips, no bumps, no lumps. Just good average responses to the checks and balances of a physical examination. Apparently not allergic and not given to common respiratory ailments. Bob and I can regularly thank God for our good health.

Death does not seem imminent. It always shocks me to learn of the death of a healthy friend of mine. Seldom do I consider myself a likely prospect for the TV commercial where the Prudential men in white coats come to escalate their prospects to the next world.

Accidents

The first major confrontation was New Year's Day 1964. Bob had gone to the Cotton Bowl game in Dallas. A friend had died during the holidays, and I was walking down our "ski-slope" driveway to ride to the funeral. (The driveway was still slick from one of our famous ice storms and impassable for automobiles.)

Somehow, it did not occur to me that it might be impassable for pedestrians also. Down I went, pride and all. Slid the last portion of the driveway with some lack of feminine style. On to the mortuary to be a friend to the grieving loved ones. It did not occur to me that this might be the beginning of a series of falls: large and small. Consequential and inconsequential.

How does an MS person drive an automobile? Very carefully! How do I drive the borrowed new Buick of my sisterlike friend? Very, very carefully. Nonetheless, while pulling out of the small shopping center in 1965, I failed to see an oncoming car until it broadsided her Buick. Indelible thoughts ran wild through my mind. Why did I fail to see the other car? Was the other driver hurt? Why did it have to be someone else's car? Obviously, I was not hurt much . . . except my pride.

How was I going to cope with this instant trauma? Apologize to the other driver. Call the police and the insurance company in that order. But what do I tell Bob? The truth hurts but usually not for long. The trip to traffic court frightened me. And wouldn't you know it? Bob was out of town. The fine was minimal, but I felt so alone when whispering "Guilty as charged." The insurance company made restitution for everything except my pride. I cried. When Bob returned, he was objective about the whole scene. But what I needed was some subjective forgiveness and grace. Yes, I cried over a small collision. Maybe those tears cleansed my spirit for the long haul of long-term illness. But what about the fear of driving? I always heard that you should get right back into the car. I did. It worked.

Falling off the bed is not a public affair, so it preserved the ego. But it raises the haunting question, will I continue to fall off the bed? Insomnia has begun with less reason. Bob was at the office. (Isn't your house usually empty when you need help?) On the trip from bed to floor, I hit my head on the corner of the lamp table, cutting open a gash on my head. The fright of the fall must have anesthetized me. The pool of blood on the carpet brought me back to reality. I telephoned a friend who was a nurse, and she arrived in five minutes. A quick trip to the hospital emergency room, five stitches, and two hours later I thought I ought to call Bob and tell him of the excitement of the day.

So far the accidents have primarily been party talk. By 1976, the house falls had accelerated. Between lack of balance and rebellious muscles, I found myself unexpectedly moving floorward more often. Frustrating, but not crippling.

The bicentennial year brought all kinds of celebration and some consternation. Arthritis had gathered around my knee. This increased the house falls. When I fell on my side, this caused rib separation on two occasions.

If you have avoided separated ribs, breathe an extra prayer of thanksgiving. (If you have gone through this ordeal, you know that every breath hurts like putting tension on a bone fracture.) But that pain, too, will pass. Later, we discovered that a fall was not necessary to separate my ribs. While in Blacksburg, Virginia, to visit Linda and Michael and to see their new house being finished up, Bob carried me across the muddy yard. Result: my shoes stayed clean, but my ribs separated again.

The first serious accident came in May, 1976, while going out to dine. The spring shower made the streets slick. We drove to the hotel underpass, and Bob was opening the car door to help me out and steady me on my cane. He asked if I needed further help, and I declined. Just as he was pulling out to park the car, I slipped and fell partly underneath the car. I remembered via nightmares for weeks seeing the back wheel of the car coming towards my face. My scream alerted Bob and averted real tragedy.

The car stopped, and I remember having excruciating pain in my hip. But it was the pool of blood that frightened me. We felt we could navigate to the hospital emergency room quicker than we could get an ambulance on a rainy Saturday night. Two accidents clogged the normal ten-minute drive to the hospital. The circuitous route of fifty minutes had its mixed emotions. Pain seldom precipitates tears and crying for me. But this was a bit unusual.

Amidst the hassle of traffic and the scalp laceration that was still flowing freely, I turned to the feminine characteristics which bring out the best in us ladies in times of stress. I flipped down the sun visor (with the "vanity" mirror and accompanying makeup lights) and shocked Bob one more time by exclaiming, "I've got to pull myself together. I look a mess. Here I am going to the hospital, and what will they think happened to me?" Out came the comb, lipstick, and facial tissue. After some cosmetic first aid, I announced, "That's better. Now I feel ready for the emergency room."

Diagnosis: broken left hip, requiring total replacement of the left hip. Thankfully, the head wound was only superficial. I wondered how much you bleed from a deep cut! MS tends to complicate most physiological malfunctions. My limb muscles can not take long periods of inactivity. They just can not adjust. X rays, consultations, drugs, and the decision to replace the hip. On to the operating room, recovery room, and back to the hospital room.

This happened six weeks before our long-planned and awaited family trip to the 1976 Olympics in Montreal. We had the condominium rented in northern Vermont. Bob says that my first words to him while coming out of the world of anesthesia were, "We're still going to the Olympics, aren't we?"

Believe it or not! Arthritis can collect about a plastic hip. We were in consultation with the orthopedist whether to suffer through another hip operation to relieve this irritant. Above all else I decided I did not want to go through another hip operation . . . and worse yet, the recovery. With this decision made, I must learn to live with pain.

My "crystal ball" failed me again. It did not reflect that within a month (February 1979) I would fall in our bedroom. The trip to the hospital was not nearly as exciting this time. I fell near the same lamp table. I called Bob and he came quickly and we went to the orthopedist's office. It did not hurt like the first fall. And no blood. So we thought it might be only a sprain or bruise. The car had been packed for a four-day speaking engagement Bob had in South Carolina.

But a funny thing happened on the way to South Carolina. The doctor heard the details of the fall and said, "We'll need to take a look at it. But first, let me tell you what has happened in my life since I last saw you in the hospital." He took fifteen minutes on his examining stool to tell me of his recommitment to Jesus Christ. He was so excited, and I hurt so much. He had dramatically changed his life-style, saying he could not get my witness out of his mind. That was a lift to my spirit, but my leg still hurt.

Finally, my physical priorities overwhelmed my spiritual concerns, and we got on with the examination. After all, Bob was speaking at a banquet in six hours. When the doctor came back with the X rays in hand, he had the "I'm sorry to give you this news" look. You guessed it. The other hip was broken in exactly the same place as the first.

Same operation. Same hospital. Same recuperation. Same frustration. Same loving friends. Same devoted husband and family. Same medical bills. Same complete recovery. (Both physically and financially.) But most of all, the same constant companionship of Jesus who kept reminding me that he had suffered himself and would be with me through my illness. Forever.

And how do you cope with accidents? Obviously, you cannot anticipate them, or they would not be called "accidents." Several lessons learned are worth passing on.

1. They, too, will pass.
2. God allows any of his children to suffer as he allowed his only Son to do so.
3. Healing usually comes to those who wait.
4. There are opportunities to witness in a hospital that you will not have in any other environment—like the Jewish family across the hall. When Bob attended the father's funeral, they asked why we seemed to have such a positive outlook on life. It gave us an opportunity to send them a copy of the "Good News for Modern

Man" edition of the New Testament. It was inscribed, "The words of this book and the teachings of Jesus can give everyone a positive outlook on life."

5. What if you are alone in the house when an emergency arises? Would you be immobilized, maybe lying on the floor and unable to call for help? If you are not concerned about such a possibility, you can be assured your family and friends are concerned. Inquire in your community for an alarm system that you can activate with an electronic button on a necklace. An ambulance or medical alert team will be at your home in about ten minutes. Well worth the cost for the peace of mind for everyone.

6. Give your friends and neighbors an opportunity to help. Loving care during recuperation should not be limited to your relatives . . . even if they are close enough to assist. Friends can patient-sit, house-sit, send thank-you notes, prepare meals, and the like.

Illnesses

Infection of the urinary tract: What's so unexpected about that? What woman is there that does not have intermittent cystitis? Several visits to the urologist in 1965 produced little encouragement for my chronic condition. An MS patient is susceptible to various secondary illnesses stemming from malfunctioning muscles. The diagnosis was that the bladder muscles could not fully eliminate the body's liquid waste. Logical. Acceptable. But quite conditional, in my case.

In July, the following year, we had invited Bob's brothers and wives to be our guests for a week of vacation. Everything was in readiness, and expectations were high. Friends had invited us to the lake the weekend prior to the reunion. What a time we had, especially riding the speedboat, bouncing on the wake of other boats in the water. Little did we know what the next twenty-four hours held.

During Sunday School I felt ill with fever and sent word to Bob that I would drive home. He would catch a ride after worship. By the time he arrived my temperature was 104°. The events that followed made a roller coaster ride tame by comparison. A general surgeon joined our family doctor at the emergency room. Something was radically wrong in the urological functions. It called for a specialist in kidney extraction. But our urologist was out of the city. Had we seen any other urologist recently? (Long pause for a low moment!) Yes, but Bob had dismissed him because of apparent lack of concern with my case. Would we mind if he were asked to do the emergency surgery? Any port in a storm . . . any appropriate apologies necessary.

Within three hours the benign kidney had been extracted, and I was in the recovery room. But what about the family reunion? Both families were already on their way from Kansas City and New York City, might as well come to celebrate the nephrectomy. It was the easiest entertaining I ever did. I received them during hospital visitors' hours, and ladies at the church brought two meals a day to our home for everyone—except me. I gorged myself on broth and jello.

After the first week of hospitalization, we dismissed the private-duty nurses because ladies of the church would take four-hour shifts to care for my nonprofessional needs. They would welcome friends at the "No Visitors" barrier and share information and caring concerns. They also helped me to share my faith by arranging the get-well cards on the walls in the form of a cross and an *agape* fish. All of the nurses, doctors, and aides recognized the meaning of the cross. When they raised some curiosity about the fish symbol, it was my entrée to share Christ's love for me and all mankind.

Our surgeon was not only medically skillful, he was a prophet. He said it would take about two years to regain normalcy of kidney function for an MS patient. He hit it right on the twenty-fourth month. How did I cope with a prolonged recuperation? Day by day with liquid intake noted—the same way one must cope with any hurdle in life—gratitude to God for healing graces, skillful medical teams, loving family and friends. Most of all,

thank the Heavenly Father for the divine planning process that
provides an extra kidney in the event one fails.

In 1979, I had an encounter with tic douloureux or trigeminal
neuralgia. Sounds almost romantic, doesn't it? Well, romantic it
isn't. It is neuralgia carried to the nth degree. Medical journals
characterize it as the severist pain known to man. And I add,
"known to we women who know how to bear pain." First, I
thought it was a toothache. One root canal and one extraction
later proved both the oral surgeon and I were mistaken.

The pain comes from who knows where and departs when it
chooses. It resembles the severest toothache, but it is more pierc-
ing, forcing the whole body to shake involuntarily. You feel normal one minute. The next minute you are driven nearly to
unconsciousness. I wish it would put you in such a state. And
what stimulates the nerve to such errotic action? A touch of food
in the mouth, water on the gums, even a breath of wind on the
cheek. It came the last time while I was still in the hospital
recovering from the second hip surgery. The pain from the surgery
was mild compared to the gyrations of the trigeminal nerve. Double doses of demerol slowed the pain some, and morphine made
it tolerable. My system could not tolerate morphine for a lifetime,
but did I want to go back to high-risk surgery while still in the
hospital recuperating from a hip replacement? A dim choice. As
Bob and I were discussing the option, the nerve set off another
series of pain. That did it. I was not willing to live with superabun-
dant pain plus the frustration of not being able to anticipate or
tolerate such pain. Bring on the surgery!

Enter our neurosurgeon friend. He transferred me to another
hospital with a specialty operating room and the performing of a
new surgical technique: damaging the nerve by overheating it so
that it could still function in all of the muscles on one side of my
face; yet, damaging the nerve fibers to the extent that the pain
would be tolerable.

Wonderful. A God-send. An answer to prayer—but there was
a prepayment clause in the surgical contract! In order for the

surgeon to know how much to damage the nerve, the patient had to be alert and sensitive to signal the absence of the tic's pain. The surgery had to be done without anesthetic. The process required nine probes into the nerve centers to damage the nerve enough to kill the pain but not so much that it could not function.

How do you cope with that much pain? By faith and prayer. Faith that God never forsakes his children. By praying without ceasing that He will give you spiritual strength to act upon your faith. Intense chronic pain does not have simplistic responses. It tends to bring you face-to-face with your Maker. How fortunate you will be if you are on speaking terms with him! If you have several wishes to make in life, consider one of them to be the avoidance of tic douloureux.

Humor finds its way into most every situation in life, except tragedy. And tragedy only has roots in things eternal. An example of such humor has its setting in romantic Niagara Falls, Canada. Only a year ago from this writing, Bob and I were visiting some of the missionaries in New York State. Sandwiched in between the two weeks of traveling was a weekend at the falls planned for our sheer enjoyment. How pleasant! How restful! How beautiful! How unexpected was our stay! Rather than two days as tourists, we had two unplanned weeks with me as a patient in the hospital.

Humor and spiritual insight are not necessarily incompatible. During the preoperative hours in the emergency room, the most unusual vision came as clear as a motion picture drama. Amidst the pain and uncertainty of moment-by-moment existence, I felt positioned between this world and heaven. The beauty of heaven was beyond description: calm. serene, bright, very bright, attractive and appealing. God spoke although not seen. I recognized his presence, praised him, and told him how ready I was to come. His words will never be forgotten: "I am not ready for you yet. I have other work for you to do on earth!"

Soon, a surgical attendant was administering a final sedative and rolling me off to the operating room. Before I knew it, Bob was hovering over the bed rail assuring me everything was OK, and God's grace was sufficient. Little did he know of my firsthand conversation with Him. It was ten days before I felt secure enough to even tell my husband of such an encounter. But it was so. And so I did.

Lousy minivacation, great maxi-opportunity to witness to our faith. Everyone felt sorry for the American tourists stranded in a foreign land. But it had its rewards. Bob did not have to be concerned about his office work or housekeeping. All the extras that go with hospitalization at home. While I was recuperating, this gave a normal opportunity to share my faith with the doctors, staff, and patients. Bob was serving as unofficial chaplain of the third floor, west wing. The local statisticians claimed we set a record for incoming and outgoing long distant calls, floral arrangements, and greeting cards. Just a bit of bragging, you say? I hope not, for it was God's way of getting the attention of some professional medical personnel who had lost touch with the Great Physician.

Then, there was the "miracle of the flowers." By the end of the first week, more flowers had arrived than the room could hold. We decided to share them with patients on the floor who had no flowers. When Bob took an arrangement into their rooms, it was a miracle to them. But miracle of miracles: the next day would bring *exactly* the same number of new arrangements as we had given away the day before. Fresh manna every morning.

God did some of his mighty works in those days. In two weeks, we flew home to Atlanta after celebrating our only night on the town atop the revolving restaurant fifty-five stories above the falls. Quite a few eyebrows were raised as we wheeled out of the hospital for dinner on the eve of our departure for Atlanta.

But why? We had come to the Falls for a minivacation. Why not take it on the last night? An understanding physician knew we could handle a little matter like that for a few hours. He'd been through the "valley" with us. He wouldn't dare keep us off the "mountaintops."

9
Coping as a Homemaker

"Opha, do you still keep up the house?" (Well, not like I want to. It seems to keep getting ahead of me. But, yes, I do my own housework.) "How do you manage to prepare the meals?" (Very deliberately. It takes more planning and preparation time than it used to take.) "You don't mean to say that you still do your laundry? I thought your machine was in the basement." (It is. It just takes two hours to wash and dry one tubful. I take something to read or mend. Or the basement and train room can always use a clean-up touch. If my strength permits, the ivy by the basement door gets a trimming.)

These are regular questions that must be fielded with regularity. Most of my friends and acquaintances see me in my wheelchair. (Remember, when away from the house I must use it for mobility. I use the walker about the house.) They naturally begin to wonder how I cope with the everyday reality of being a homemaker. For most women today, homemaking is a sideline, an avocation, even a necessary evil. For me it is basic, my vocation, the headwaters of fulfillment.

Then why is it so frustrating? So regularly and predictably frustrating? I guess it is because it takes at least three times longer to complete any task than it would for a normal person. Again, I am reminded that my condition is not normal. And being a homemaker reminds me of it time, and time again. For that is what it takes to keep our home: time. It takes two hours to "whip" up a light supper, three hours to straighten the house: countless hours to clean it.

And where is the fulfillment in that? It is deep-seated in my

115

being. Mother breathed into me the saintliness of homemaking. She was such a model of succeeding under difficulty. (At least I don't have to help operate a farm before sunup and after sundown.) In the division of labor on the farm, my tasks were centered about the house and garden: cooking, cleaning, gathering stove wood, and tending to the chickens. How fortunate! Maybe my parents knew that I was petrified by the animals, and my oversensitive nose could not tolerate the barnyard. Whatever! Even though I was born on the farm, I was raised about the home believing that making it a haven was a calling of God.

Before MS, I could make our home in the snap of a finger and still have time to be active outside the home as noted in earlier chapters. As MS became a reality and long-term illness became a live-in factor of my life-style, what mid-course correction could I make? Would I just let the house go unattended? Brow beat the family to take up my slack? Employ full-time help? As I projected the logical outcome of these (and many other) alternatives, they produced some fantacies, some dreams, some nightmares.

Sewing has taken a diminishing role since the girls left home: Some mending here, some skirts adjusted there, some drapes altered. Making dresses is out of the question now. Somehow I missed learning to knit in the earlier years, and it has become a therapeutic, challenging hobby. Afghans are slowly completed but worth every stitch. Sweaters are out of the question.

Some people do not see me as competitive enough. Maybe they are right, maybe not. I do not choose to waste my time and energy in petty competition such as losing sleep over the failure of my favorite athletic teams, being seen in the right place with the right people at the right time, or feeling that I must be a trend setter in fashion styles. (But I want to be a trend follower and be somewhat in style.)

But try me out on competing where life values are at stake. My tortoise qualities generally persevere to outlast the hares of the world. The determination to make a home worthy of the name is one of these contests.

Victory requires substitutes and pinch hitters, game plans, and halftime strategies. Innovations and cancelations. Since I cannot shop the home shows, it means gleaning the home magazines for new ideas and economic remodeling. It means choosing sturdy furniture and fixtures (with a touch of class) since I do not have the strength to replace furniture. We can afford rearrangement better than replacement. It means learning to eat left-handed. Bob calls me a "switch eater." The switching takes place countless times a day.

Prioritizing became a necessity before it became a catch word of the political and business worlds. After the girls were out of the home in the early seventies, I found my ideas for home improvements were in apparent conflict with Bob's. We discussed the differences. Argued them. Yet both of us held to our preconceived notions. These "no contest performances" produced "no winners." Eventually, we just stumbled into a simple remedial process. (Bob always says it is better to be lucky than smart.)

Each of us listed on tablet paper our top ten preferences for home improvements. The lists were dissimilar in general and in specific. Then we took time to explain why each of our listings were important to us. (It was interesting that the lower two thirds of both lists could not be as enthusiastically defended as the upper one third.) Next, we reprioritized our preferences in terms of what seemed best for us as a couple rather than as individuals. Amazing results! We had both rearranged our priorities to such an extent that the top ten were all inclusive on both lists. And the top four were identical. (Another case of practicing what we had been preaching! For years, we have advocated to newlyweds that they recognize the value of the union of their marriage over their individual likes and dislikes.)

Handicaps need not stifle creativity. They fan and stimulate it. Taken-for-granted situations come into the refining fire of reality. I had to find new ways of doing old things. Often this meant willfully forgetting how it used to be done. Wishful thinking is a long way from hopeful planning. Trial and error became my scientific process.

The barriers of steps, distance, and strength are indeed formidable. But so are barriers of picking up things that my weak hands inevitably drop, reducing the trips between the refrigerator and the stove, calculating the least energy between two points or two functions, deciding that the dishwasher does not have to be operated at a certain hour daily, making peace with minimal dust on the furniture that I used to say was "an inch deep," preparing food in advance and freezing it for who-knows-when occasions, placing chairs so I can move from right to left when sitting. The list could go on and on.

Chief Cook and Bottle Washer

You often hear couples give accounts of their first conflict following retirement. The contention is not over the purchasing of a new car. Usually, it is something like the husband wanting to reorganize the kitchen cabinets similar to his organized office. Long-term illness is a type of "retirement" for the homemaker. And along comes Bob with his knack of organization. What a collision of ideas! Bob brought logic to the issue, but it was the logic of a person without handicap.

One day he had efficiently rearranged the cabinets to my total consternation. At the price of extra space he had stored often used items at the rear of the cabinets—just where my weak hands could not reach, nor my weak legs bend or kneel. In desperation, I finally said to him, "If you won't try to reorganize my kitchen, I won't try to organize your office!" One helpful thing evolved. We installed pullout shelf trays which enable me to sit on the chair and quickly lay hands on the needed items.

An ounce of planning is worth a pound of cooking. I just don't have time or energy to do things a second time. Nutrients need to be considered, volume accounted. Try to plan dinners to be used twice: fresh and frozen. Many "begin from scratch" recipes have been scratched. The "pinch hitter" is prepared with easy-does-it mixes, adding my own pinch of this and that. Trying one new recipe a week is fun and adds a bit of excitement at the dinner table. If it fails to taste up to my expectations, I add some ingredients when the leftovers are served later in the week. Bob calls me the "Queen of the leftovers."

Small cans and quantities help in the planning of small meals. Since we got over "maltuition" as the girls moved out on their own, convenience has taken priority over economy.

However, we become conservative when grocery shopping. As needed we shop the sales and buy in large quantities. Bob pushes me in the wheelchair, and I push the cart. (We must look like a double trailer going down the aisles.) The extra food is stored in the basement freezer and pantry shelves. An accurate inventory is kept up-to-date in the kitchen. The trip down the basement stairs is too laborious for inaccurate inventories. (I also combine such a trip with a laundry venture.)

Bob does the necessary shopping early Saturday mornings. He claims he likes to do it when the stores are uncrowded, so he can have his coffee and donut while locating the items on my grocery list. But he hasn't convinced me that he gets up early on his only day to sleep just for his convenience! Now and then I drive to the super-market to pick up items previously overlooked or recently needed. This means shopping at the least crowded times, finding a store where I can park in front of the door. Accepting help from stock boys and friendly shoppers saves energy by going to the yonder parts of the store. Oh, it takes me sixty minutes to do what others could do in thirty. But it makes me feel like I'm in the swing of things . . . doing my own thing.

I Don't Do Windows

Cleanliness and godliness may go together, but limited energy complicates the equation. Fortunately, Bob enjoys a neat home environment and is willing to do his share in making and keeping it neat. But we had to compromise on what constituted an acceptable level of neatness. One day of outside assistance every other

week became the solution. Mattie, Lucile, and Marie have been
my helpers during the last two decades. More than just helpers,
they have been soul sisters. We have ministered to each other in
more ways than chores and wages. Not one of us did windows.
Bob doesn't clean too well, but he does windows.

In the earlier days each daughter had daily and weekly tasks.
Basically, they did the evening and weekend dishes, Saturday
chores, laundry, vacuuming, kept their rooms picked up, and
some outside yard work. To their credit they did it effectively and
cheerfully. One of the advantages of long-term illness is that family members recognize the need to pull their own weight. My
decreasing eyesight makes it easier to settle for something less
than spotless perfection. I never did like washing windows. Now
I have an excuse.

Just as games are won with pinch hitters, pinch runners, and
other substitutes, they are also won with better equipment. As
muscle deterioration took its toll, I had to find tools to meet my
needs. Creativity was needed. There was no laundry shoot. More
expensive houses seem to have them built in. Fortunately, our
central bathroom is directly over the washer and dryer in the
basement. We cut a hole in the closet floor and presto: laundry
shoot. The broom closet formerly held a broom, mop, and selected
cleaning tools. Now it holds that and a multitude of other
household helpers that generally are housed in a basement: ham-
mer, screwdrivers, nails, screws, extension cords, gardening and
plant tools, masking tape, sprays, pans, and handy gadgets galore.
The things that I can fix must have the tools nearby, or I lose my
enthusiasm before I get started. Why not wait until Bob gets
home, you ask? Oftentimes that is several days away. Besides, of
such daily chores my therapy is composed, both physical and
mental.

Sweeping the kitchen floor is relatively easy. But sweeping the
dust into a dustpan is laborious, at best. One day while browsing
a catalog for "Helps for the Handicapped" I came upon such a
simple solution: a long-handled dustpan. So easy, it almost makes

it fun—almost, but not quite. The heretofore mentioned "kangaroo pouch" attached to the collapsible walker is invaluable in carrying so many things, so many ways. Another step reducer is to have small household items collected in several places about the house. Perhaps the key is to have usable supply items as near the use area as possible.

Gradually, I became a very organized homemaker. I have lists for everything: groceries, drugstore items, hardware, thank-you notes, weekend chores for Bob, extra cleaning for my biweekly helper, calendar appointments, a telephone list that rivals the Atlanta Southern Bell directory. I seldom kept lists before MS. I thought it was an insult to my memory recall. The encroachment of the aging process and the imperative of energy efficiency have redirected me.

Homespun Maitre d's

There has always been something special about breaking bread together. As a family unit or within the larger family of God. Maybe it was first impressed upon me as a child when the preacher's family usually had Sunday dinner with us. Perhaps it was Bob's family get-togethers, at home, or eating out in Kansas City. Maybe God ordained it when he placed soul and stomach within our body walls.

After Bob and I had a few dates I invited him for dinner to the apartment. I always enjoyed cooking for others, especially for those who seemed to appreciate it. As our girls grew, conversation became mutually stimulating. We lingered at the table after dessert, sharing opinions and dreams. I felt that the food, tastefully prepared, attractively displayed, and carefully set on each place had something to do with setting an environment conducive to warm fellowship.

Entertaining came naturally. I would have made a good maitre d'. We inherited Mother Bingham's Bavarian china and crystal. Bob brought a set of Noritake china home from Japan following World War II. The churches we served showered us with fine silver at Christmas and anniversary times. As a working girl I saved enough to purchase my flat silver. Wedding gifts filled in the cracks of supplying us with the accoutrements for delicate dining. How fulfilling it was to have guests in for dinner, candlelight and all. (The candles were tolerated by the menfolk at least until the appetizer plates were picked up. It takes more light for men to eat.)

Would MS eat away at our social dining? What adjustments were needed to prevent it? While we obviously could not continue at normal entertaining, we decided that cutting down was better than cutting out. Sometimes, entertaining out was a substitute for entertaining in. Maybe the occasion called for an invitation for dessert only rather than a full course meal.

Some other refinements included cutting back on the number of vegetables served. No self-respecting farm meal contained less than four choices plus at least two salads, maybe two kinds of breads and desserts. My conversion from rural to urban life cut the selections in half. MS further reduced options. Five courses could be cut to four, and three when less formal. Even with these labor-saving decisions it takes one or two days to get ready to prepare a dinner for six.

Bob assists in getting all place settings on the table the night before reluctantly agreeing to cover the settings with a cloth to keep the dust and air pollution from the silver and china. The rewards of preplanning pays off by using foods that can be prepared and frozen a day or two before. To my surprise homemade rolls could be frozen for ready use. Certain commercially prepared foods have been developed to such a state of the art that they taste home made.

No longer can I serve the table. My struggle to do so seemed to create tension for our guests. It is easier to let Bob do it. His attempts at the social graces are always sincere, even if humorous at times. The lady guests always offer to assist, and sometimes I give in, basically, because they desire to lend a hand. I'm not fooling myself to think the quality of the meals are up to my old standards. Maybe God adds his own taste and spices to the ingredients. No one seems to refuse our invitation of second helpings.

Cleanup time has always been easy. Bob agreed early on if I prepared any meal, he was willing to clean up after it. Of course, that meant a few more nicked glasses and chipped dishes. The flatware was not prewashed thoroughly before he put it into the washer. The pans were not spotless but generally were "foodless." And the fact that he truly enjoys helping me makes up for male fastidiousness. When the guests have said their last good-byes, I am ready to cave in for the night. The clink and clatter of the dishes being washed are sweet sounds to the ear. His whistling tunes are harmony to my soul.

In spite of my attempt to cut back on the food put on the table, we still have appropriate leftovers. "All of the hungry children in China" still call out from my childhood. What to do with the leftovers? Economic and energy levels mandate they be recycled. Maybe my most consistent attempts for creativity have surfaced here: a little spice here, a bit of sauce there, add a garnishment, think up a French name. Presto, yesterday's leftovers become today's cuisine a la Opha.

In recent years we have specialized in election parties, anniversaries, and functions organized around the Sunday School classes that Bob and I have taught. There are needs for small-group activities and training that are made noteworthy by breaking bread together. These occasions are usually simplified by asking each lady to bring a covered dish. Then we have the best of both worlds. Bob still gets to clean up, and he still claims to enjoy it.

Take Time to Smell the Roses

How much energy can I expend on yard work and flower gardening? That is like asking how much nourishment the soul needs? I can remember how a few flowers and a trimmed hedge turned a dust bowl farm into a diamond set among withering corn crops and vegetation loaded with grasshoppers.

Before MS I enjoyed being the yard lady of our home. The girls were not old enough, and Bob was not interested enough. Amidst the babies and bottles it was good to have a mix of flowers and fertilizer, shrubs and shears, cuttings and clippers. Bob did the grass.

And what about today? It's just one more in a train of frustrations. I simply can not find the time or energy to maintain a flowery yard. Yes, it bothers me. It cuts back on my aesthetic values. Sometimes I want to throw aside my walker, race out the back door, skip up the steps to the rock garden, and do my thing. Experience has taught me that such fantasies are brought to the screeching reality of broken limbs. But I must be able to take a recess from the routine grind of dragging one foot after the other. I must be able to stop and smell the roses.

What compromises have been made in this, another area of daily compromises? How much can a person compromise? As much as needed! You learn to do a lot of things you never thought you would have to do. Call it adjustment. Call it coping. Call it whatever you want. It is not pleasant, but it is far better than giving in to nothingness. Determination and flexibility are my constant companions.

Here are some attempts with which I have been able to make peace amidst frustration. First, I delegated the responsibility of the yard to Bob. I would be the supervisor. He knew that would not work. It took me four years to believe it. In the meantime, he began to "enjoy" gardening if it came without supervision. (What is it with men that they resist supervision?) Regardless, as I was able to be less "bossy" he was able to be more helpful. He says he enjoys it now; he is even willing to take some advice, carefully given. I still choose the flowers and places of their planting. Clipping the ivy along the rock garden wall is a weekly chore. The rest is up to him—and God. Come to think of it, maybe that's why Bob has been open to change. God does wondrous things, his miracles to perform!

Second, we altered the topography of our backyard and reduced the task. We planted the back two-hundred feet with pine seedlings and left it natural. The small, level area up to the house was developed into a large patio. Small rising steps with a wrought-iron railing get me atop the retaining wall and into the rock garden. Flat stepping-stones amid the lawn were hard to traverse. The change to a curving cement walkway with matching railing provides the ease of mobility to walk from back door to driveway and rock garden.

Third, my flower cultivation was reduced from many plants to a few hanging baskets and a couple of potted varieties on the patio. This allows my touch on them from planting to cuttings.

Fourth, I still can not tolerate weeds regardless of who is managing that part of the yard. Bob indulges my prissiness and takes supervision rather stoically. (What else can you call it when he grumbles silently!)

Fifth, there is more therapy in passivity than I had imagined. Sitting on the patio, I can experience so much of God's creative wonder. A wide variety of birds come and go. Small animals scamper about the trees and grounds. The constant greening of the pines delights me. The colors of flowering bushes glow amid lush green grass. It is some ego trip for one to feel it necessary to have had a direct hand in the cultivation of it all before she can enjoy it at all.

Sixth, just seeing the woodpile assures me of many nights about a glowing fireplace. I have learned how to build my own fire when Bob is out of town. He brings a few small logs just outside the sliding doors to the patio. By carrying one log at a time in my pouch, I can set a small fire. We installed a gas jet to ensure that the logs ignite. The ash drop was installed to simplify the cleanup. Can you feel the exhilaration of building a fire on my own? It almost makes up for a day of struggle. Almost . . . but not quite. You have to experience the struggle to be able to make the comparison. But both are worth "taking time to smell the roses."

Telephone as a Home Companion

Sounds like a commercial. Maybe the copywriter for the yellow pages had long term disability. We have often felt the telephone to be the most enjoyable utility. That may be because we have never gone for extensive periods without water, light or heat. Be that as it may, the telephone is a real companion for me. Here are some examples.

● It is a quick locator for my shopping needs. Since I cannot go browsing any more, I need to know what is available where. The yellow pages reduce the options, and a call to the merchant verifies the merchandise being available and suitable.

● Ask the small, corner merchant to meet me at the curb with my order at a mutually suitable time. You would be amazed at the cooperation and pleasant response. It is almost like I am doing them a favor. Terrific energy saver!

● Early, we put an extension phone in the bedroom and later, one in the basement. Only recently have we installed a cordless phone which I keep in my pouch. (Do you get the feeling that the pouch gets overstuffed?) Having the receiver quickly accessible solves many problems. The least of which is that many callers hang up on the fifth or sixth ring. It was maddening to finally reach the receiver only to have the caller hang up or, worse yet, to stay on the line without answering.

● Local calls are a necessity. Long-distance calls are a luxury. But there must be some trade-off for missing so many other of the joys of life that you normal people take for granted. I needed to talk with mother in her nursing home in Missouri. How I wished I could be nearer to physically minister to her needs. That being impossible, the next best thing was to talk with her at least once a week. A few minutes covered the bases and brought a happy feeling at the sound of her voice. Just visiting with one another gave a needed sense of security to each of us.

Talking with Nancy in the city is rewarding and is spiced up with her visits to our home. But the calls to Linda's home span the 400 miles that we only travel about twice a year. With the grandchild beginning to verbalize her affection, I hate to predict what the long-distance charges will be. But they'll be worth it!

Is it worth the cost? Compared to what? All of us have our excesses. How can you compare the conveniences and luxuries above with so many materialistic expenses? I can't, and I hope I'll never have to do it.

General Prescription for Coping as a Homemaker: If God gave you a talent to be a homemaker, you must use that talent, or it will be taken from you. If any part of your family remains in the home, you may be best equipped to make your home a haven . . . or a heaven. It is a God-given outlet . . . and he will bless and multiply your efforts.

10
Coping Within the Community

One of the throwbacks to my rural childhood is that everyone ought to know everybody in the neighborhood. There were all of thirty families within a three-mile radius of our home. And a mobile society was unheard of. Between school parties, church functions, building raisings, and grain thrashings, everyone knew everybody.

But Atlanta is light-years from Lockwood, Missouri. The local school unit is still a viable way of getting to know your neighbors. The church units are seldom geographically oriented. The other factors are nonexistent.

Getting to know everybody in the neighborhood was frustrating enough before MS. It is almost impossible with a debilitating disease. "Who is my neighbor?" became more than a Bible story for me as I became less mobile. Social normalcy is fed at the wellsprings of social contacts. One adds to the supply of spring water by meeting and helping others.

Fortunately, I had countless neighborly friends at church. Some of them lived fifteen to twenty miles away, so they did not totally fill my need for knowing geographical neighbors. Through the years I trust that I have been able to relate within the community as they have ministered to me.

In the Neighborhood

• We invited the neighbors to a New Year's Drop-in. Since our house is not commodious, and crowds are a deterrent to my mobility, we staggered the hours of invitation on December 31. (No need to compete with the bowl games on New Year's Day.

129

Besides, I wanted Bob to show up.) The actual fellowship was good, but the unexpected benefit was taking the initiative in being neighborly. For months people on the street would wave and express appreciation for the party, or renew regrets for missing it. The media was the message.

● Inviting ladies for informal tea has helped. A phone call is all that is needed to make it happen. It is my pleasure to have tea or coffee and cookies ready. Conversation comes naturally. And it helps to remove the mystery of the lady who drives up the street with the wheelchair strapped on the back of the car.

● Returning smiles for stares was not easy at first. Often, I found myself refusing to make eye contact. When I did, they would be staring and quickly look away. Smiling comes naturally for me, so I just smiled and spoke. Greeting with a smile becomes contagious, not to mention therapeutic.

● Personal visits to our neighbors are almost impossible. Our street is hilly in all directions and impedes foot travel even to the hale and hearty. But the mailman takes my little notes and cards, and the telephone lines are reliable save for famous Atlanta ice storms. When a personal appearance seems necessary, I can drive up the neighbors driveway, even if it be next door.

● For the close neighbors we have enjoyed entertaining them in our home for a meal. It is revealing for them to notice as this MS person struggles, but it gives me a chance to show what the old girl can still do! Different neighbors dictate different dinner settings. It's an outdoor cookout for the three single young men with whom we are cultivating a Christian witness. But it is more formal dining for our other neighbors who are seventy-year-old friends from New York. There is nothing like breaking bread together to break down the artificial barriers we humans create.

● Perhaps I am one of the most reliable "watch outs" for neighborhood burglars in the community. My "at home" situation provides watchful eyes for neighbors where all persons work. It has a reciprocal effect when Bob and I travel.

● Baking cookies provides entrees to old and young alike. The kitchen fan carries the delicious aroma outside. Very soon neighborhood children drift towards our kitchen. One lad very regularly carried a handful of warm cookies to his home. His embarrassed mother telephoned, "Opha, I've just scolded Theo never to ask for cookies again." Creative lad was he. His opening line changed to "Mrs. B., something for my hand?" Other contacts with the younger generation were provided by teaching them to play board games and asking them to do some yard chores: modest pay for modest work.

● Twenty years with the same next-door neighbors was a mutual blessing. Many were the opportunities to practice our "Christian Neighbor Policy." We miss these neighbors as death has entered each home. However, new neighbors in each house bring new opportunities.

● Speaking of new neighbors, that is my special time to send Bob with a pan of fresh-baked breakfast rolls their first morning. And offer to help them get acquainted in the neighborhood, as well as to find the shopping places and professional services. This might be classified as casting "bread upon the waters" (Eccl. 11:1) for any neighborly kindness has been returned on the incoming tide.

In the Schools

Growing up attending a one-room elementary school added an appreciation for public education. There is value in the system, and we always supported it. Our moment of truth came in the fall of 1962 when our Atlanta schools were to be integrated. The national media came. Over five-hundred strong, to report the anticipated fracas. The churches announced 7:00 AM prayer services as a peaceful demonstration of support for integration. I thought it was worth any personal physical struggle for me to support the school's endorsement of human personality.

Both girls, Bob, and I were in church that morning. You may recall that God answered the prayers of concerned, caring people. It was worth the effort. Not a newsworthy encounter was reported. The prayers of the righteous "availeth much." And our public-school system provided a high academic standard for our girls.

● Having to give up the normal motherly duties of room mother, paper collector, and project sponsor made me look for other avenues of service. I telephoned many neighbors and asked them to save their old newspapers for our girls to take on the paper-sale days. (Guess whose classes always won the prize?)

● Attending school PTA was easy. But attending lunch with the girls on special days was a challenge. Often it required advance planning to circumvent stairs.

● Why the Brownie leader seemed to call for assistance at the most opportune times perplexed me for awhile. Finally, Bob admitted that he telephoned the leader when my physical dexterity would allow such participation. "Opha, could you bring cookies and drinks, Thursday?" It meant so much for me to be involved in the girls' activities.

● I got even with Bob by calling the principal and volunteering his services. Our extensive travels coupled with his photographic experience and educational know-how provided the teachers with a natural curriculum enricher. What are wives for if it isn't to volunteer projects for their husband?

● Attending the honor banquets required early arrival to get a seat near the rest room and tuck the walker or wheelchair out of view.

● College was not a time to let down. Perhaps it was the time of greatest support. It meant semiannual trips for parents day and holiday activities. It included special phone calls when the football team won and "sympathy cards" for the tough losses. Of course, money from home was a welcome surprise. It seemed that I received more thanks for an occasional ten dollar bill than their father received for tuition, housing, and food. Who said life is fair?

● Perhaps the greatest physical demand involving the school took place during the national presidential election of 1964. (We voted at a neighboring school.) We were warned about a large turnout in our precinct. So we took a folding chair and some reading material. Little did we expect a three-and-one-half-hour line. You can be sure there was ample time to get acquainted with neighbors.

• In the last few years I have used the absentee ballot. This is easily obtained by checking requirements with the office of voter registrations in your county.

In the Church

It has never been a temptation to reduce my church relationships since I always receive more strength than it takes from me. God and his committed children seem to have overflowing cups of love. It is distressing to hear people say they are too busy or too tired to worship. He has never been too busy or too tired to support my needs. His emotional and spiritual refreshing comes with each worship experience. I can ill afford to use MS as an excuse.

• We make plans to arrive early enough to get settled before others arrive. This not only calms my muscles, but it conditions my nerves and spiritual sensitivities.

• There were unusual urological adjustments following the kidney operation. (Bob called me his "go-go girl.") It necessitated placing a chair outside the sanctuary door near the loudspeaker system, so I could come and go as I needed.

• Discipline was often a problem while teaching sixth graders. God supplies strength in wonderful ways. I prayed for physical strength for the task. He provided with extra spiritual strength, also. Women at their best are not a physical match for active twelve-year-olds. But these pupils respected my spiritual resources, and not one problem appeared.

• When making house visits with a coteacher, she would walk in front of me to distract attention from my halting walk. Early planning prevents so many frustrations and eliminates exhaustion upon arrival.

• Once a month on Missionary Day, Bob leaves the wheelchair inside the church door on his way to work. At a later hour a friend drives me to the same church door. From then on it is easy. The involvement with other ladies in the study and planning of projects is stimulating to soul and mind. "Yes, I will prepare the chicken casserole for twenty-five senior citizens the last Thursday in the month." A friend offered to pick it up at eleven o'clock that morning. Bob picks up the chair on his way home. Necessity is indeed the mother of invention.

● There are many outlets in the church to provide physical and emotional therapy. Most churches are begging for help. Ablebodied persons may have the option to volunteer or not. But those of us who are confined desperately need adult fellowship, not to mention the feeling of worth to the community and the Kingdom. Many activities are too active. I need time and flexibility to effectively participate. Especially helpful has been telephoning for information, surveys, overdue library books. Serving as a volunteer librarian is a once a month responsibility while the administrative tasks of our Sunday School class are weekly and sometimes daily assignments.

● Bob and I had always belonged to a large, organized, functioning church until recently. Last year, we helped to form a mission congregation about ten miles from our home (about twenty times as far as the church we belonged to for twenty-two years). Now that is an experience. It takes a bit more of everything, but how rewarding. It not only requires about three round trips a week but visits to prospects who live near the mission church. But I had forgotten that small congregations without church hostesses need soft drinks mixed, cookies baked, summer missionaries housed, and frequent covered dishes for suppers.

The congregation has doubled to about sixty now but not without blood, sweat, and tears from every person. It was so difficult to give up the ease, comfort, and closeness of our mother church. Not to mention the fellowship of close friends for many years. But isn't that what sharing the good news is all about? Aren't we to go into every nook and cranny of our nation . . . and our world . . . in a wheelchair if necessary? You bet your life! Christ bet his!

General prescription for coping in the community: a case study on the question "Who is my neighbor?" A couple with two girls once moved next door to us. They were Southern, white, and Baptists. Good neighbor prototypes? He was preoccupied with his business and flowers. When not traveling, he had little time for his family. She secluded herself and gave little time to her kids. The pieces were puzzling until we learned she was an alcoholic.

How does one relate to these "neighbors"? Their girls required our attention. The family indeed had problems.

Who is my neighbor? Anyone who needs my help. Their younger daughter was only five at the time. She found it difficult understanding her environment. She obviously needed a "mother." Now that was something I could do. It often meant preparing an extra plate for dinner or taking one more passenger to Vacation Bible School.

Would I have done the same for a Northern, black Catholic? You bet your Samaritan stamps, I would!

SECTION THREE

The Keys to Freedom

11
Faith: The Glue of Hope

People often ask me, "What makes up life? What are the real ingredients that enable you to keep going?" That is one of the ponderables for every age. Are they asking what seems to separate humans from animals? Or are they asking among humans, what is available to all of us that so few of us seem to appropriate? Probably the latter.

I would like to think that I had an answer uniquely mine. But many of you would readily recognize that my answer was written nineteen hundred years ago by the apostle Paul. In his counsel to the Corinthian church, he condensed the great qualities of life into: "Faith, hope, and love . . ., these three" (1 Cor. 13:13, RSV). Through some dark nights and lonely days I have tried to add a quality or so to these three. But my addendum seem to pale in the shadow of "these three" making mine seem to be parasitic.

Settling on Paul's trilogy, I began to consider the order in which they are given in 1 Corinthians 13:13. While there are other options to the sequencing, the biblical order seems to be most logical to me, considering my experience with long-term illness. I began with faith: "the substance of things hoped for, the evidence of things not seen" (Heb. 11:1). Then came hope: that positive and optimistic swelling of the soul that can overcome and stare down depression. Lastly, abides love: the most Godlike of all our finest characteristics. Faith and hope have their beginnings and endings. But love is eternal.

Faith: Primacy of the Spiritual

Who am I to try to explain faith when the giants of ages have carefully iterated and reiterated the facets of this gem of life. I dare to put my ideas into print only because they are mine, born and tested in the crucible of life. If you are theologically or psychologically trained you may have a field day in higher or lower criticism. While noting the incompleteness of my observations, please remember: I give them only in answer to the second question-sentence of this chapter.

My "edition" of faith has not been blind: simple, yes, but not unmindful of the facts of life. Reasonable, yes, but one often gets to the limit of one's ability to think things through. Open, yes, but carefully screening the bizarre ideas that are loose in the world today.

An overstructured faith seems to be an encumbrance for the soul and a maze for the mind. I cannot fathom the labyrinth of details that compose the faith patterns of some notables in our society. My faith is simple. But it has been systematic for me in that it has pervaded my whole being. Childlike, yes, in that when I have no more choices available, I must make some decisions on faith alone.

It has not been a magic wan. If so, I would have waved it years ago to the advantage of my health and any other needs that I have not been able to remedy. Unexplainable? Yes. Magic? No.

Foundation of Faith

When condensed to its lowest common denominator, my faith is centered in the characteristics of a sovereign, loving God. It is hard to write this portion of the book because I am not theologically trained. So grant me some experiential license.

1. God **created** me. He, like a good father, loves those whom he has created.

2. He **cares** for the birds of the air. How much more he must care for me!

3. He **provides** for those whom he has created. The ecology of the earth indicates that the higher the creation, the greater the provisions.

4. He is **omniscient** and knows what is best for me even though his long-term view mystifies my myopic vision.

5. He is **omnipresent** whenever and wherever I need him. No out-to-lunch God is universally available.

6. He is **omnipotent.** Like the elephant, he can do whatever he wants. Unlike the elephant, he always does it right.

7. He is **sovereign.** My whims and whines will not change the mind and spirit of the Ruler of the universe.

Therefore: if he creates, cares, provides, is all-knowing, always available, all powerful . . . am I not in good hands to commit my life to his will? Sounds simple and somewhat logical to me. Why is it then in my weaker moments I still wonder why? When? Why? Where? Why? How? Why? Don't ask me. I am waiting to ask him in that day when I meet him face-to-face. Happily for me, those questions will be answered (anthropomorphically) walking about heaven on healthy legs.

You surely must be asking upon what authority did I frame the seven factors that frame my faith. First, they are based upon the Word of God as interpreted to me by his Holy Spirit. Not necessarily as interpreted by my helpful pastor(s) or some national religious figure. Before I could sort out a faith to sustain a long-term illness, I needed a foundation that would not crumble under the weight of my needs.

By faith, Abraham was sustained. Likewise, Isaac, Jacob, Moses, David, Samuel. The New Testament pages are filled with persons who literally put their life on the line for Jesus. Martin Luther discovered in Habakkuk's prophecy that the "just shall live by his faith" (Hab. 2:4) while driven to his knees for penance. And Martin Luther King provided me with a contemporary role model. I rediscovered this truth as my knees could no longer function.

Second, faith became a leg of my trilogy of life when I observed it in the lives of others. Obviously, there are the internationally known giants of the faith that have impressed so many of us. But the ones to whom I refer are those unknown to the pages of the *New York Times*. But they are known to me personally. I watched them with scrutinizing and discerning eyes to note if they could pass through the waters without drowning or, maybe more important, without abandoning their heretofore claimed faith.

I wish you could have known my parents and how many times I have reflected upon their faith. And my pastors and Sunday School teachers, and other church leaders. Oh, they had their shortcomings. But they came up with long suits when the chips were down. Remembering back over the four church relationships that I have known since married life, it has been good therapy. Geoffrey Swadley, the pastor who officiated at our wedding, demonstrated how to love his enemies and those who spoke all manner of evil against him falsely.

M. O. Land, a wealthy merchant in Saint Joseph, lived the life of humility. Charlie and Betty Shacklette faithed it through the separation from their child born with incurable brain damage. Nanny Ruth Sargent showed how to bear up under the death knell of cancer. The Ernest Garretts exhibited unbelievable determination in making good things happen amid a difficult environment. Taffy Moore traversed the deepest of the valleys only to come up on the other side a stronger Christian. Joan Turner was able to draw upon a faith nourished through several terms of foreign mission service in order to put her trauma-filled life back together.

Third, my faith concretized when I internalized my own experience. God has walked and wept with me every step of my way. He allowed me to piggyback my weighty problems on his back. Sometimes he just picked me up and carried me along. Other times, he felt it best that I limp on my own halting gait. But all the time, I knew he was doing what was best for me. Some valleys have been deep. Some mountains high. Some sorrows too hurtful to easily recall. But not once did I feel him ill equipped or unwilling to give his sovereign attention to my needs. Thank you, Father, it was always your will and not mine that I needed to be done. Therein lies my faith: "Oh, God, give me one step more."

Related to Healing

Perhaps more than any area of life my faith has been put to the test relating to why God has not yet healed me. Maybe you thought earlier that the end of the story would be a miraculous healing and restoration. So do I. From the diagnosis through today, I feel that surely God has the divine trump card to play. As the Jews awaited Messiah, I await medical relief.

When muscular restoration did not come in the early 1960s, it was decisiontime for me. In chapter 3, I mentioned that giving up was not my nature. But how will I react if things are not going to respond as I want? Without fanfare I decided that no matter what comes, I want to be a Christian witness. By word and by deed.

Many a lofty proclamation has eroded on the anvil of time. Yet I was sure that I could maintain my goal, come what may. Well, "May" came, and so did June, July, August, etc., multiplied by many years. But medical restoration, not a bit. When long-anticipated relief does not arrive, it surely tests our faith.

Divine, lightning-quick intervention did not seem to be God's will. What about faith healing through the channel of medicine? Earlier chapters gave an account of my search. Always words and paragraphs of hope. An isolated case history here, a retraction of earlier reports there. Research is improving, but it's a long trail to follow if they have not yet discovered the cause of MS . . . let alone the cure.

Enter the possibility of faith healing through the person of a minister. I didn't know how to handle that one for sure. There seemed to be as many valid reports of genuine healing as there were dubious reports. Every profession has its quacks. Was it a challenge of my faith? Was it a possible oversight to the answer God had waiting for me? Was I timid, afraid, proud? What a shame that such a span of emotions should parade across my psyche. Several friends referred to me persons who gave credible testimony to their experiences.

Right or wrong, I decided to be available for such a miracle of healing. But I would not seek it out. During the process, God helped me to see the possibility of using such human instrumentalities if he so chose. I still hope for such a blessing. And I hope it is not immodest to state that I know I have the personal faith to catalyze such a healing . . . if God so wills it.

In at least two ways I am a product of the miracle of God. First, the neurologist that diagnosed the MS prognosticated that I would be an invalid bed patient in two years. Second, only one area of the complex physiology of my body has failed to function. The remaining kidney is A-OK. Both artificial hips are still functioning. The weak bladder fights off infection daily. The trigeminal nerve tic has not reappeared. The annual physical checkup is routinely beautiful. And most of all, the miracle of keeping my mind and spirit in a healthy condition.

Job's Friends

By far the most traumatic challenge to my faith was the well-intentioned advice from "Job's friends." The Bible recounts the story of a good man who came upon very hard times. His friends observed his grief and told him that if he had not sinned, God would never have afflicted such pain and sorrow upon him. That being the case if Job would repent of his sins and ask forgiveness, God might give him a second chance.

Job's friends must have many great-grandchildren. You may still hear or read about them. Even as we prepare this manuscript, a valet parking attendant means to be helpful when he says, "Don't worry, lady. If you just praise God and live right, you will be cured." Beware if they come to the door of your soul. Always have a "Not at home" sign ready for quick display.

You never know when you might encounter one of Job's friends. On a night when a quiet and carefree meal was called for, we went to an East Indian restaurant. Not likely we would meet any acquaintances there. We needed time to ourselves. Hardly were we seated when the owner came to our table. Bursting into our privacy he inquired, "Madam, would you like for me to heal you? I have had miraculous results. All I ask you to do is close your eyes and let me touch the part of your body you want healed." So much for a nice, quiet dinner experience!

In the sixties, different people in different ways came to me with the best intentions. The details were different, but the message was the same: "All you need is enough faith, and God will heal you." What a spiritual wringer of the soul that can be! The inferred corollary is that if you are not yet healed, you do not have enough faith. Back to my knees, Back to the Bible. Back three quantum leaps spiritually.

If you would go to this meeting, read that book, fast for so many days, visit this doctor, pray this prayer. But the most difficult invitation to deal with was unexpected: "Will you let two or three of us come and pray with you? The Scripture says that when even two or three are gathered together in his name that he will answer their prayers." After several years of considering this passage, Bob and I do not feel that is what it says or means. You may not care about our opinion. That's understandable. But if one of Job's friends comes to see you, you will need all the help you can get—even ours. So put on your theological waders, and let's test the water.

What does the Scripture actually say? "Again I say unto you, That if two of you shall agree on earth as touching any thing that they shall ask, it shall be done for them of my Father which is in heaven. For where two or three are gathered together in my name, there am I in the midst of them" (Matt. 18:19-20).

On the surface it does appear that a few of us can agree on something, pray, and ask God to make it happen, and he will so act. But where does that leave the sovereignty of God? Does that mean that his will can be changed by the frequent collection of a few petitioners? God forbid! And I think he has and will. Jesus pleaded in Gethsemane's garden that he would not have to suffer a cruel death. But knowing God's sovereign characteristic, Jesus added that nevertheless he wanted the Father's will to be done.

Finally, I was able to make peace with Job's friends, the Scripture, and my own theology. It came when I realized that all petitions to God go with the assumption that all such requests are in the will of God. To carry this concept further, it is our belief that the basic prayer for any believer is "Thy will be done" (Matt. 6:10). Every other communication to God is a modifier of that base.

Now that theological conjectures are settled, why am I still asking "why?" Why has it been God's will that I not be healed? Does he not want me whole again? Surely, he doesn't enjoy seeing his children suffer or handicapped. I am willing to give him all the praise for the miracle. Being able to do more works in his name would come naturally. Why then, am I still so limited?

Revelation comes slowly to me . . . or I am slow to understand it? But once it does come, I have it. And here it is: there are millions of good Christian ladies in the world. They do many good works. They are devoted to the Lord. A good lady is not hard to find. But it is unusual to see such acts and deeds of mercy among persons with long-term illnesses. I pray that I can be the best witness possible to the love of God. He has shown me that the best way is to witness in spite of circumstances and consequences. And so he has.

Now if he ever chooses to completely heal me so I can witness to his grace in another way, I am ready. Bob and I plan to put a full-page ad in the Atlanta newspapers announcing a celebration service at our church, inviting our friends to join us in praising God for his gracious power. If it happens, ya'll come!

Relating to the Unknown

Early in my illness I began to read medical books on the physical and emotional effects of MS. How depressing! How demoralizing! The literature might be the equal of Chinese water torture. But it did one thing for me: it brought a resolve that researchers did not understand the progressive condition of my illness. If that be the case, then, why should I worry about it? That one decision must have brought more sanity for me than I can imagine.

But the best-made resolutions often go awry. When the day is dreary . . . and I am lonely . . . and the brain says "go," but the muscles say "no" . . . then it is that questions of the unknown resurface in my mind.

Will I become totally invalid? Images of case studies race through my mind. Bedridden friends to whom I have ministered. Loss of body control. Drawn facial muscles and exacerbated leg muscles. All of these pictures are powerful enough to sweep a person into the alley of doom. As mentioned earlier I determined early on that I could not let such negative thoughts consume me. Particularly, when the odds are good that I will not regress to that stage after these many years of regression.

Will I outlive Bob? Maybe and maybe not. If I do, will not the same God that has supplied my needs for all these years be competent to supply them without Bob? Life needs would have to be rearranged, and habits restructured. It will be one more bridge to cross. Bob helps me regularly to be prepared in such an event. Financial matters are reviewed. Household details are logged. Dependable repairmen are listed. He assures me that our professional friends will continue to meet our needs. We have discussed the pros and cons of keeping our present house . . . living with other members of our families . . . keeping an automobile . . . and a file full of other options. The first and last card in the file would be that God will take care of his own.

Will I be unable to serve others? Maybe if I consider only the ways that I serve people now. But there are other ways. The telephone, the mail, this book. Who knows what new media will emerge that will extend my sphere of service?

Will life become worse than death? Who knows for any one of

us? That is a theological question. Some days might. But who knows what type of death we face? And aren't we glad that we don't know? So really my dilemma in answering this question is no different than anyone else's.

Will I lose my spirit? Probably not, unless I throw it away. Throughout the pages of this book I hope you have felt the stimulation that comes from living in constant awareness that God's strength is sufficient for any circumstance in life. Take a few minutes to read Romans 5:1-5. These verses give me the assurance and peace of mind that allows me to feed and strengthen my spirit. My guess is that my spirit should continue to grow. Remember, it is not handicapped. Indeed, it is nourished and nurtured by God's Spirit.

Sharing My Faith

There come times in every Christian's life when they must share the good news or wither spiritually, just a bit. Before MS it was with some difficulty and infrequency that I was able to articulate my feelings in any manner resembling an evangelical thrust. I remember living a life that could stand close scrutiny. Not that it approached sinless perfection, but it reflected the love of Christ in my actions.

On the Christian scale for overt witnessing I would have appeared more Presbyterian than Pentecostal. If a person asked me about my beliefs, I could share my position. But I would rarely seek out someone with whom to witness. The coming of MS gave me a channel of comfort to actively tell what God had done for me. Mind you, it was not that I did not have a faith to share. It was only difficult to do so.

MS was the lubricant that made it so much easier to swing wide the door for witnessing. And what a blessing it has been for me . . . and hopefully for others. I am not timid or aggressive. Not verbose or articulate. But I do feel that I have a simple, but powerful story to tell those who need to know of the love of God as manifested through his Son, Jesus.

This willingness grew slowly as I began to put together the pieces of how God was allowing me to witness for him via MS. The pilgrimage seemed to peak when I looked at death face-to-face in a Niagara Falls hospital. From that point, I have eagerly sought opportunities to share my faith with anyone who would listen.

Maybe this is the time to let you readers in on a little secret. For about four years Bob had patiently but persistently encouraged me to write this book. Overwhelming! That was the first feeling. In all the fantasies I have ever entertained, authoring a book was at the bottom of the possibilities. An author I am not. A person who can turn a phrase? Not on your life! It frightened me to entertain the idea and still does.

Bob persisted—said my story needed to be told for the benefit of others. OK, but someone else needed to tell it. Even if they would, was it possible for me to recall twenty-some years of events? Most threatening—could I emotionally relive what had been searing to my emotions? Also, could I open the doors of intimacy to put into print what was safeguarded for my husband and closest friends?

For several years the project was rejected or at least postponed indefinitely. Bob backed off. But friends began to inquire if the writing were underway. Their disappointment motivated me to rethink the difficulties involved as compared to the prospects of witnessing to my faith.

Finally, the leap was taken. Bob helped to organize the outline, and I began putting experiences on the ever-present three-by-five cards. The day of reckoning was at hand: time to begin writing sentences, paragraphs, pages, and chapters.

It was our custom to go to the beach or the mountains for Bob's writings. So off we went: typewriter, copy paper, dictionary, three-by-five cards, etc. Actually, it was exciting! Imagine me writing a book for publication! That's a long way from Lockwood, Missouri . . . and a one-room school building.

After two days of writing attempts, only four pages were completed. At that rate, my epitaph might read:

> She tried to write
> But few words came.
> She tried again;
> Results the same.

If I had never started! Why did I give in to such pressure? Climbing the Rocky Mountains would have been as reasonable. And how could this failure be explained to the few friends who knew of the project? Just another disappointment in a never-ending line!

Gradually, my vision was cleared to see the possibility of sharing my faith more effectively through the printed page. I guess I was timid about assuming that I had a story worth writing or stimulating enough to be read. But since you have gotten this far into the book, perhaps I was wrong.

Several years passed. Maybe the project was dead and buried. The only glimmer of life in it was the need to share encouragement with other persons with long-term illnesses, their families and friends. One day Bob risked some rejection by resurrecting the subject. Promptly, it was reburied. Some exasperation surfaced to our flushed faces. My frustration and incompetence resurfaced. He countered with the option of my telling the story to him, and he would put it into words on the page. But would it be my story? He responded by saying, "You lived it. It is no one else's story!"

With that we began a two-year process of telling, writing, changing, retelling, rewriting, and editing. Speaking about "coping with the unexpected!" Who would have thought how much time and energy would be required? And I had precious little of either commodity in excess quantities.

But it took a Niagara to get me into an accelerated mode. Since then I cannot wait to get the manuscript done and to the editors, printers, and distributors—a giant leap forward in my willingness to share my personal experience in Christ. And I owe most of that incentive to the fact that I have been able to live with MS for more than twenty years. If I had been cured and healed years ago, I might have had a *Reader's Digest* or *Atlanta Journal* article. Many are cured, and it attracts only passing notice. But few there are who persevere through a longtime, lifetime illness with growing optimism, hope, and zest for life. Thanks to MS, a vision on an operating table, and an all-knowing God who chose to allow me to be his witness through suffering, that may be as close as I'll ever come to being like his Son.

And to whom has this neo-evangelical spirit been directed? As might normally be expected, towards my family, friends, neighbors, and people I have met in my life-style. No door-to-door calling or television programming. Just looking for those that God has given me.

Primacy of the Spiritual

The Bible teaches it. Preachers preach it. Why is it so hard for us to practice it? Matthew gives a significant amount of Jesus' discourse on the mountain to the principle that life is more than food and clothing. Yet when the Christian community notices a disciple practicing this basic tenet, it is surprised. And that may be the nicest adverb used to describe such action. More like odd, fanatic, irresponsible or out of style.

But not until I came face-to-face with MS did I put physical values in their proper place. They are not in last place but a long way from first place. Spiritual properties do not have to contend with moth, rust, or thieves. It occurred to me that the sphinx may have had a long life . . . but only a day in the time of eternity.

Sounds like a sermon doesn't it? If so, it is one that I need to hear myself. For it is the basis of coping with a disease that gradually destroys the body. My mind must regularly remind my soul that my body is not primary. Life is infinitely more than flesh and blood, muscle and myelin, and creature satisfaction. It is basically a matter of the spirit.

But greater personages than I have declared the axiom, most of them with their lives in blaring testimony: Paul of Tarsus, Savonarola of Italy, Gandhi of India, Wallace of China. Why then, am I as one crying in the wilderness? It is because this basic tenet should be foundational to all Christians. But it may be a matter of life therapy to those of us who travel the rocky path of long-term illness. For along that path I learned that flesh and blood really do pass away. Only the spirit is eternal. That is a league in which I can participate without handicap—free at last. Thank God, I am not incarcerated by the physical.

Maybe this is why Bob and I chose to donate our bodies to medical research upon our physical deaths. We hope it will be a testimony to the supremacy of the spirit over the flesh. We hope it will be a reminder to the community and a legacy to our family that our bodies are as dust. Rather than a grave to symbolize the capturing of our bodies in a box, we trust a memorial service will testify that a grave could not hold the Christ within his body. If you are in the vicinity, do come and celebrate my home-going to the Father. And my release from a body that so long has been so limited. May a memorial service help my family and friends to celebrate my victory over illness and death.

I do want to be remembered for that part of my spirit that reflected my Lord: caring for others. Humility, forgiving, triumphant attempts in scorn of weakness. I still am determined, no matter what comes, to be a Christian witness in word and deed. Lest it appear that I think I have arrived, may I invite you into the inner sanctum of my prayer life? Laced among my poorly phrased petitions are two pleadings of the early apostles: "Lord, teach us to pray" (Luke 11:1) and "Lord, Increase our faith" (Luke 17:5).

General prescription for living with faith:

> Let me fast when needed;
> Let me feast when needed;
> Let me have wisdom to know
> When to do what.

12
HOPE: The Balm of the Soul

Hope seems to be a double or nothing affair!

Philosophers through the ages have waxed eloquent on both extremes: optimistic and pessimistic. It has been called grief's best music, at the same time phrased as the most hopeless thing of all. Unless seen through a Christian perspective, it can be the soul of the unhappy—a kind of a cheat. The atheist Nietzsche said it was the worst of evils, for it prolongs the torment of man. For me, it has been more like Brunner described it: one of the ways in which what is merely future and potential is made vividly present and actual to us.

Hope must be a first cousin to faith. In rereading the last chapter, many of the traumatic days' struggles were relived. *Faith* and *hope* are horizon words that expand the mind and give toughness to the spirit. Particularly do I recall the second hip break. In one way it was routine. A second time over the same route. Same doctor, hospital, nurses, therapy, predictable recovery. With one exception: Would I ever walk again? I remember telling God that I had to walk again, for there were miles to cover and reducing years to make the trip.

Between meals, transfusions, catheter, medications, and niceties of the hospital routine, I came face-to-face with immobility. If the first artificial hip moved me from the cane to the walker, would the second one send me on to the wheelchair permanently? The doctors usually can take their "smart" pills and give an odds-on prognosis for the alternate limb replacement, but not with MS. That is one of the multimysteried parts of the disease. Would the hip's artificiality significantly impact the other muscles of the limb into further rigidity? Would the already weak muscles reject the plastic inset of ball and joint? These questions raced through my mind for days and nights.

Hope comes in varied packages. Some theological. Some emotional, some intellectual, and some practical. Maybe the latter could be called "instant" hope. When being rolled into surgery for one of the hip operations, I remember hoping that the surgery and its attending enforced recuperation would not further retard my mobility. Cutting through the huge thigh muscle and keeping off my feet for several weeks usually would take its toll from an MS patient.

It was two weeks into convalescence. In the therapy room an elderly lady had a similar operation. (It was not ego satisfying to learn that broken hips were usually relegated to older persons, much older.) She was refusing to try any exercises because "they hurt too much." Actually, she confided to me she had no hope of walking again, but the therapist advised otherwise. In speaking to the patient, I tried to share my faith and hope with her to no avail. After seeing how lack of hope eroded her spirit, it eventuated in a redoubling of mine.

There was another time when hope was the balm of my soul. Contemplating a long life with long-term illness is a poor substitute for waking up each morning, well and whole. It is the climate in which to write songs of the blues. It engenders overtones of the blahs that are expressed in hit tunes like "Is That All There Is?" and "Send in the Clowns."

I was sitting with Job amid his ashes. Only my questions were phrased differently. How long, oh Lord? Will I walk again? Why can't I be free to help others? But eventually questions surfaced akin to Job's. "Why must the righteous suffer pain?" and "If a lady die, will she live again?" (see Job 14:14).

Some deep waters must be crossed alone. Jesus' pleas from the cross came to mind, "My God, why hast thou forsaken me?" C. S. Lewis's preface to his book *The Problem of Pain* has a quotation for help in such times: "The Son of God suffered unto the death, not that men might not suffer, but that their suffering might be like His." In the last analysis, one must decide how deep is the river, and can I cross it?

Such a time was the prospect of having my hip surgically re-broken in order to alleviate the pain from arthritis around the prosthetic ball. The option was to accept the probability of increasing and debilitating pain. Neither option was acceptable. Maybe another hip operation would put me in the wheelchair or bed permanently. But increasing pain brings no hope either. Reason and logic have their places. Faith stands high in the characteristics of the spirit. But there comes a time when you must step out into the deep of the river . . . hand in hand with hope.

Medically, the hope that sustains me is that medical research will discover a cure for MS. Emotionally, hope is to be able to see it through. (You menfolk, I believe, call it "tough it out.") But spiritually, the greatest hope for all long-term patients is that God will miraculously bring healing. If not to me, to others.

We often read of the "slave syndrome." Such a condition has tight bonds, linking strange bedfellows. Perhaps handicapped persons are caught up in that syndrome. Our freedom is restricted by many physical and psychological barriers. In certain ways we live in a bondage as sure as the slaves of Babylon, Egypt, or Colonial America. Certain places are off limits. Some experiences are relegated to recall of the memory and not to be repeated again. The future can be tightened up to here and now, with a possible peek into tomorrow.

The music of the Negro spirituals has always been enjoyable to me. Foot pattin'. Head swingin'. Hummable tunes—we sing them about the house. Used them as the spirit of camp-fire services. But it was not until I needed some extra measures of hope did I begin to understand the heart of most spirituals. It seems to be hope. That ability to trust in a waking dream of what could be. It is desire and expectation all rolled into one. A charmer for every woe.

You remember some of the songs: "Nobody Knows de Trouble

I Sees but Jesus," "Soona Will Be Done Wid de Troubles of de World," "Swing Low, Sweet Chariot," "Steal Away," "Deep River," "Didn't My Lord Deliver Daniel?" "Every Time I Feel de Spirit," "I Wanna Be Ready," "Lord, If I Got My Ticket Can I Ride?" "Soon One Mornin'," "There Is a Balm in Gilead," and "Ain'a that Good News?" Just recalling the collection gives me hope for today, tomorrow, and forever. Spirituals were the original "soul music."

As the disease took its slow but systematic toll, hope became the token for the toll-house. Note the varying degree of depth (or shallowness) contained in the plateaus. Observe that an ounce of hope could produce a pound of determination. In collecting the research for the book there seemed to be several plateaus of hope.

First, the diagnosis was faulty. A reasonable basis for hope. It happened frequently twenty-five years ago with MS. So much so that diagnosticians were very hesitant to assert any finality to their opinions.

Second, that it would go away. It came as a mystery, maybe it would leave likewise. If the research lab cannot isolate the cause, maybe there is not a disease, and it will in effect vanish.

Third, it would stabilize early. Case histories gave reason for such hope. A few acquaintances of ours had a history of MS, but you could hardly notice it. No matter, if I could just have a 10 percent increase in my muscle control, surely I could make it.

Fourth, I would be miraculously healed. Perhaps this did not come earlier because I wasn't significantly handicapped. When medicine, therapy, and wishing had not brought normality's return, I could resort to the hope of the miraculous.

Fifth, research would discover the cure. This and the previous hope come intermittently. Maybe it is the no-man's-land between reality and the miraculous.

Sixth, I would be able to see the girls through their education and weddings. Almost sounds like plea bargaining with God. But it was hope. Hope that was translated into life . . . which encouraged me to hope again.

Seventh, I would walk again. Throw away the walker and slowly put one foot in front of the other with enough balance to keep upright. This may fall into the category of hoping against hope.

Eighth, that I could stay well enough to travel some with Bob. His business traveling has been a plum to our coping together. If I became homebound, it would be a double blow: no more diversions to my routine life and additional loneliness because of his absence.

Ninth, that I could hope for continuing remission. Actually, the longer I live the more likely the condition will become stabilized into remission, if I just knew that I would get no worse.

Tenth, I could keep on keeping on!

You may recall the Beatitudes have a structure of plateaus built into their sequence. Beginning with humility and teachableness, they move on to more difficult characteristics. The above plateaus are not to be compared with the Beatitudes, but they do progress to higher levels of response and growth.

What is there about hope that almost makes her a fickle suiter? Like a lover who continues to make enticing promises but produces sparingly, if at all? But at the next promise the hopeful one sees a pot of gold at the end of the rainbow. But what would have happened if Lady Hope had not sent some rain into our lives? No rainbows?

When constructing the "what-if" scenario, we must take a hard look at the "what-if-not" alternative. To be sure, hope does not always come through. But what if she were not there at all? Then what? Would it have been twenty-five years of despair and depression. If hope builds upon hope, doesn't despair multiply despair? Surely it is better to have hoped and lost than never to have hoped at all.

What about my present hopes for today, tomorrow, and forever? At the risk of letting you into the closet of intimacy, let me share some of them with you. My batting percentage may not be any higher than the past. But if I can reach .400, I'll be at the top of the big leagues. And who knows, some of my hitless slumps in the past may tend to increase the odds for me in the future.

My hopes for the future:

(1) That faith will sustain my attitude.

(2) That the poet was right: "The best is yet to be."

(3) That present and future barriers can be met with courage and good judgment.

(4) That continued support can be realized from spouse, friends, and the medical profession.

(5) That I can relate as a whole person to our granddaughter.

(6) That long-term hospitalization can be avoided.

(7) That any disability or bodily malfunction will not be a family burden.

(8) That this book will be helpful to others.

(9) That as I try to give hope to others, it will extend my horizons.

(10) That long-term illness will help me to separate the wheat and chaff of life, allowing me to put first things first.

(11) That the cause and cure will be discovered by the researchers, and medicine can be prescribed for prevention and recovery of MS.

What Is Hope?

What is hope, that man is mindful of her?
Is she the impossible dream?
A mercy ship anchored beyond my grasp?
A terrible hoax played out in the blues
   of the world, destined for disappointment
   at best . . . and depression at worst?
                              No!

What is hope, that I am mindful of her?
   She is the most likely link between
      reality and eternity.
   A small foothold on the sheer cliff of
      the struggle for a life more than
      existence.

A shaky bridge that may not carry me across
the chasm but will not drop me into the
abyss.

Yes!

What is hope, that I put my trust in her?
She is a dependable friend in the darkness of
night.
A spirit of achievement in the brightness of
day.
A way to put my hand into the hand of God.
A chance well worth the risk.

Selah!

ROBERT E. BINGHAM

13
Love: The Greatest of These

I *hope* you do not have a superstitious *faith*. If so, you may have problems with my using a chapter thirteen for a *love* chapter. But remember that Paul's great love letter came in the form of "chapter 13."

The veterans of faith probably memorized this high watermark of the Scriptures as a child. Others of you may have studied it as classic literature: the crowning essay on the subject. Whatever your introduction to these divinely inspired words, let me attest to Paul's judgment that love is the greatest of all human characteristics. Greater than faith, hope . . . or any other collection of valued traits.

In the event you are not familiar with his words, or do not have a Bible available, let me take a page to set this passage before your eyes. If you have it memorized, maybe you know the words but might be missing the meaning. Why not read them again? This time, see if God does not have a special word for you in the context of living amid difficulty.

A library of books have been written on this passage. Biblical commentaries have devoted pages of scholarly interpretations. However, it may be that your spirit has not been receptive prior to this time. Your approach may have been academic, or your felt need was not hurting enough. Whatever your case, I feel led to set these words before your eyes again. Perhaps, you will want to pause and ask God to give you unusual insight into the meaning of Paul's letter to the Corinthian church of the first century.

If I speak in the tongues of men and of angels,
But have not love,
I am a noisy gong or a clanging cymbal.
And if I have prophetic powers,
And understand all mysteries and all knowledge,
And if I have all faith, so as to remove mountains,
But have not love, I am nothing.
If I give away all I have,
And if I deliver by body to be burned,
But have not love, I gain nothing.
Love is patient and kind;
Love is not jealous or boastful;
It is not arrogant or rude.
Love does not insist on its own way;
It is not irritable or resentful;
It does not rejoice at wrong,
But rejoices in the right.
Love bears all things,
Believes all things,
Hopes all things,
Endures all things.
Love never ends;
As for prophecies, they will pass away;
As for tongues, they will cease;
As for knowledge, it will pass away.
For our knowledge is imperfect and our prophecy is imperfect;
But when the perfect comes, the imperfect will pass away.
When I was a child, I spoke like a child,
I thought like a child, I reasoned like a child;
When I became a man, I gave up childish ways.
For now we see in a mirror dimly,
But then face to face.
Now I know in part;
Then I shall understand fully,
Even as I have been fully understood.
So faith, hope, love abide, these three;
But the greatest of these is love (1 Cor. 13:1-13, RSV).

There are other worthy translations, but this is the one that I have read literally hundreds of times. I was raised on the King James Version and put it to memory. It was foundational to my faith. But Bob had given me a new Bible for Christmas 1964. To compliment my well-worn KJV, he selected the Revised Standard Version. Whatever the form the substance is the message, and it came from God.

The greatest of the Christian dogmas for me is a sentence of only nine letters: God is love. Too simple you say? Perhaps, but broad enough to describe the essence of God. And basic enough to be biblical. "He that loveth not knoweth not God; for God is love" (1 John 4:8).

While writing this manuscript it occurred to me that to want to be loved is like God also. Perhaps we consider that the need to be loved has selfish overtones. Sometimes we tend to grasp for love at another's expense. But does not the Bible teach of God's desire for his children to show their love to him? If God in all his might and strength needs love, how much more do we need love? And for those of us who have seen our strength ebb away, we seem to thrive on love. Perhaps it is best expressed by accepting persons for who they are rather than by what they have, or what they can or can not do.

"The strongest weapon of all against MS is love." This statement came not from the laboratory of science or from the cathedrals of faith. It came as the last line on the last page of a little book, *Future Unknown - A Family's Fight Against Multiple Sclerosis,* written by Donald Key, a patient with MS. As a professional journalist with the Cedar Rapids *Gazette,* he has taken over a hundred pages to tell his story well. I underlined many ideas and options. As I pulled out the book to scan it again, I found my own comments in the margin. After the above quoted sentence, I found my handwritten "Amen!"

This experientially founded precept was also given to me as a prescription for MS by our neurosurgeon. After unsuccessfully trying several medically acceptable drug treatments, he said, "I believe the only thing for you is a large and consistent dose of love from your family and friends." The prognosis was prophetic.

Love from Parental Family

Most of us were blessed with caring parents. The human race would become extinct except for this God-given nature of parents. But long-term illness can distort this normal care relationship into an abnormal selfish one. Being unable to accept the illness for what it is, the parents often look for someone to blame. That cloud of guilt can blow up a real storm and finally land on an innocent party. It can be any member of the family or those closely associated to the family. Never mind what are the physiological facts about the disease or accident. Parents can easily become "Job's friends."

Not so with mine. Sophistication and erudition are not twins of the Ozarks. My parents and siblings brought a minimum of these qualities to bear upon any issue. But they brought deep spiritual understandings grounded in faith . . . hope . . . and love. And these three bore acceptance of me as a whole person. To be treated as a normal member of the family. Not pampered nor coddled. Neither avoided nor isolated.

How did they show their love? Let me count the ways. By the depth and breadth of love their souls could reach. And just how did they reach me 800-plus miles away? In ways you would expect of people raised and bound to the land they cultivated.

Simple things, but not to be taken for granted. Things of invaluable worth touched my soul like two letters from "home" a week, in addition to the weekly newspaper from Lockwood. No anniversary event ever passed without a greeting card to commemorate it. Just for the record, I should say that Mom and Eunice (sister) were the correspondents. Dad and Hubert (brother) did not take to the pen easily. They were always included in those who "sent love."

But when fall came around the menfolk came through with the family's annual Christmas gift: a side of western fed beef. What a nice way to wrap up your love in a package of prime beef! It lasted the year through, and each piece was unwrapped in love. When Dad died in 1969, we assumed that would be the end of the "care packages." Not so. Mother and Hubert have continued to stock our freezer with meat. You may miss the point of this generous fall tradition. It wasn't the value and savings on the groceries that was so tasty. It was the week-by-week reminder that my family cared for me and mine.

Then there is the fireplace. You may remember that one of our two prerequisites for an Atlanta house was a fireplace. But Atlanta houses with fireplaces did not come in our price range. Several years later when the folks were visiting with us they heard me say how much we wanted the warmth of a winter fire in the den. Rather than give us the money, they gave a greater gift: faith. They lent us the money to have that fireplace and chimney built into our den. And further showed their faith by telling us to pay it back when we could. In the meantime, we were to remember them each time we sat in front of the fire. What a legacy! They gave us the joy of many-splendored feelings around a glowing fire and the memory of the love of parents. It makes you feel good, doesn't it? But can you imagine the support it gives me when depression tries to stick his ugly head into my mind! Day in and day out the remembrances that I am still loved by those who nurtured me through those early years. Time and distance were not barriers.

Earlier this year Mother grew weaker. She had become terminally ill with several organs malfunctioning with cancerous growths. Yes, it has bothered me to be so far away and physically helpless to help the one who took me to her breast many times beyond the weaning days. Again and again, God has provided. In those times, it was Hubert living and ranching the home place. Going by the rest home to see mother every day of the year. And Eunice driving down from Kansas City every other week to give the feminine touch. In both cases they not only served Mother, they supported me. I desperately needed to know that my mother had a support system worthy of her years of investment in her three children.

Eunice has been available to nurse me during post hospital visits. Dropping everything, she would be on the airplane as soon as it seemed feasible. You know how it is: just to know that your loved one *wants* to come means as much as having them actually come.

Love from Immediate Family

You have read references to their support in the preceeding chapters. Even between the lines you could not have missed the vital role each of them has played. But this section serves to isolate some specifics. Perhaps they will serve as helpful suggestions for you who are family to someone with long-term illness.

When you see your strength diminishing each week, each year, you need someone to give you long-term stability. Bob has lovingly given just that—consistently. And that is a characteristic money cannot buy. In the fourth world of uncertainty, stability is a condition to be sought from one's spouse.

Two types of illustrations can be appreciated: the deep abiding expressions of love and those small impromptu indicators that mean so much to those of us who need affirmation. The long-term expressions from Bob have been: (1) practicing fidelity to our marriage vows; (2) providing financial security; (3) demonstrating Christian leadership for our family life; (4) accepting my condition without indulging me; (5) willing to compromise our differences; (6) wanting the best for me, and us; (7) planning to keep our marriage exciting amid the reality of MS.

How often have you said that it was the little things that made life so sweet? Let me assure you that sweetness is nice, but sometimes we need something just to make life palatable. When I feel that I cannot go another day with legs of stone and icicles for fingers, Bob comes through with an impromptu expression of love. Some that have been therapeutic are listed here:

(1) Telephoning in the middle of the day just to ask how the day

is going and to tell me how much he loves me. (2) Lunching together once a week, when possible, at a place of my choosing. It's almost like dating again. We actually set the dates each Christmas week for the following year. (3) Treating me like his lady and not a handicapped person. (4) Showing special kindnesses to my mother like sending regular notes and cards. (5) Taking me with him as much as possible plus giving me the option not to go. (6) Helping around the house. Just his helping to keep the house orderly is a blessing. (7) Kissing me each time we separate or reunite, be it for the day or for a week. It's not perfunctory. It's love!

Each daughter has given supportive love, each in her own way. Having been forewarned about overparenting teenagers, we had no way of knowing how they would react to my accelerating MS. They responded with more maturity than could have been expected. Perhaps their greatest love gift was choosing not to be rebellious. Recently, they volunteered they had nothing to rebel against! You will never know how rewarding and reassuring those words were to my ears.

Some specifics: (1) Performing their chores about the house effectively and pleasantly. (2) Volunteering to assist in any way, any place, any time. (You may think this is overdrawn. Perhaps they acted out their humanity with others, but they were consistently unselfish with me.) (3) Leaving little love notes about the house; now that they are grown, sending those messages by phone or by mail. (4) Showing respect for the values and traditions that our family holds dear such as the Christmas Eve worship service in our home. (5) Offering to help with errands that would fall my lot. (6) Accepting my illness matter-of-factly rather than one to be avoided.

In proofreading this portion above, it almost seems too good to be true. No family is that perfect, true. Ours is not perfect. But we have chosen to be our best when coping with my illness. Obviously, we have acted out our imperfections in other places with other people.

Without medication to handle my MS, can you imagine how my family's love support is vital to my physical health? Not to mention mental health?

Love from Friends

Most of our friends are within the family of God. But there are neighbors who join this group in looking and finding ways of showing their love. These range from volunteering to pick up some grocery items to anonymous gifts to help with medical expenses. This provided therapy not covered by medical insurance and substantial supportive aids for handicapped persons that we could not afford. Each time these help me about the house, I thank God for the love of an anonymous donor. Often friends take me to medical and dental appointments when Bob's presence is not mandatory. Again, it is not the act itself that sends the vibration of love. It is the thought and feeling behind the act.

Telephone calls and friendship notes are heartwarming. Bob says that I have a corner on "note sending." But it does me good to laboriously type out my messages to others. And just as much fun to drive down to the mailbox and find some correspondence from friends: bread on the water.

It's so easy to tell how much people love you. Dogs can always tell if you love them. And we mortals are smarter than dogs. True, some folks have a hard time in expressing such emotion. But given enough time, they come through. If only we knew how therapeutic our acts of love can be to others, surely we would follow the apostle Paul's prescription printed earlier in this chapter.

Love from God

When all is said and done, our love for one another is based upon God's love for us. If not, our love is fragile and fleeting. Not that non-Christians are incapable of love. They just do not have as strong a model as Jesus of Nazareth. It is the *agape* love that roots us.

God has revealed himself to me with some degree of clarity

since I was a child. Since MS my vision of his revelation has been a bit clearer, yet I'm still seeing "through a glass, darkly." Daily devotions are as regular with me as they must be to Benedictine monks, and certainly just as vital to my existence. They are not routine. They are life sustaining. They are not "sixes and sevens." They are "sevens and elevens."

In such multithousand contacts with the Father, it seems so simple to recognize that God is love: and love is God. Rather than try to share my experiences of divine revelation, why not let his Word speak for itself? Here are some of the biblical texts that have sustained my spirit. Maybe they will sustain yours, or you can share them with a friend who is traveling through the valley.

● "Behold, what manner of love the Father hath bestowed upon us, that we should be called the sons of God" (1 John 3:1).

● "Walk in love, as Christ also hath loved us" (Eph. 5:2).

● "Above all you must be loving, for love is the link of the perfect life" (Col. 3:14, Moffatt).

● "Since God's love floods our hearts through the Holy Spirit which has been given to us" (Rom. 5:5, Moffatt).

● "God commendeth his love toward us, in that, while we were yet sinners, Christ died for us" (Rom. 5:8).

● "So we know and believe the love that God has for us. God is love, and he who abides in love abides in God, and God abides in him" (1 John 4:16, RSV).

● Perhaps the most known, most profound verse of Scripture says it all: "For God so loved the world, that he gave his only begotten Son, that whosoever believeth in him should not perish, but have eternal life" (John 3:16).

Sometimes Greek philosophers are hard to understand. But Plato spoke for me when he wrote: "All love should be simply stepping stones to the love of God. So it was with me; blessed be His name for His great goodness and mercy."

14
Death: A Trilogy

"Who's afraid of the big, bad wolf?"

"Who's afraid of Virginia Woolf?"

Well, I can tell you right up front that I was afraid of both of these symbols of death. Most any girl growing up on a farm was taught to fear wolves. If my parent's verbalizing was not enough, the scattered remains of lambs about the farm would have done it.

And Virginia Woolf? Never met her, but the symbolism in the stage and screen play was enough to petrify me. A seductress that could mean the death of the second most precious relationship in my life: my marriage.

Most of us grew up with the threat of the "bogeyman" getting us. And some of us faced death the first time as a child through a prayer better designed for our grandparents:

> Now I lay me down to sleep,
> I pray the Lord my soul to keep.
> If I should die before I wake,
> I pray the Lord my soul to take.

For years I would hear seers and sooths of the day proclaim, "There are many things worse than death!" And I would think, *Maybe so, but name one.* Since those early days of youth and young adulthood, there have been many, many opportunities to consider these age-old questions.

For the child, what could be worse than death? For the teenager, perhaps painful suffering, torture, or long-term paralysis. For the young adult, maybe it would be solitary confinement, boredom, or infidelity. We older adults might prefer death to a long life of bedridden suffering. For MS victims might fear total dependency more than anything.

Some will say that death is too morbid to think about, let alone put into print. But that is only to suppress what may be the most-asked question within the inner sanctum of our souls and minds: "If a man die, shall he live again?" The Book of Job was the first written book of the Bible. It contains some of the collected wisdom of the ancient world. The lead character of the story sits in contemplation of his life and death and asks the question uppermost in his mind, "If a man die, shall he live again?" (Job 14:14).

You can be sure that this question has been pondered in the heart time and time again. So, this is shared with you not as the wisdom of the ages, but rather the recollections and determinations of a few decades.

God knows of our fear of death and seems to have lovingly eased us into understanding and accepting this last stage of our life's cycle on earth. Surely death is a trauma to be treated with respect. The question is: Should it be treated with fear? Most of us experienced death first through the loss of a pet. For some, this is a separation greater than a casual friend or relative. Next, may have been a grandparent. Unless this person lived in our house, it was still removed from our daily lives. Then came our older friends, mostly past their sixtieth birthdays. We were so young that they seemed ancient, and it was rather natural.

Of course, there are those exceptions that still try our faith. Just last month we received word that one of our "adopted" students was killed in Indonesia. Capable, talented, and committed Christian. Son of missionary parents. Spending a summer in his beloved land which nurtured his growing up. Yet, in a moment, in the passing of a trailer truck with his motorbike, life was scratched out. In these unusual circumstances the old question of "why" resurfaces. Bob and I have not yet worked this hurt through the processes. But when we do, the answer will be the same as it was after years of MS.

Death is a part of God's plan for man's developmental cycle. We are conceived in love . . . nurtured in love . . . find freedom in love . . . choose a vocation in love . . . perhaps choose a mate in love . . . develop to maturity in love . . . and finally, we die in love. Each step of the cycle is intended by God to be fulfilling and to be a prelude to the next step. It seems he created it to be so. And can you imagine him determining the final segment of the cycle to be disastrous? It may be interpreted by man's faithlessness to be so. But not by a loving God who has the power to make life what he wants it to be.

For years, the resurging question for man was, "Why did God put man (and specifically, me) on earth? Was it accidental? Was man a pawn on God's chessboard? Or perchance, a princess? But never a queen? What was his eternal purpose, anyway? God may be a fast teacher. Maybe I am a slow learner. But it took years to assimilate my own theology to this question. Theological scholars have written books enough to fill library rooms to explain it all. For me and my soul, it has distilled into a few sentences. Maybe they will help you find a comfortable pathway through life to life, via death of the body on this earth. If not, maybe it will point you to one of the classic books. Or to a person acknowledged to be filled with wisdom.

It seems that we were created to:

(1) Glorify God and enjoy him forever.

(2) Accomplish God's will on this earth.

(3) Decide by free choice if we want to follow his Son as Lord and Savior of our lives.

Is that too simple to fortify you in your encounters with death? Then expand it. Amend it. But, for your sake, come to grips with the purpose of your being.

Since no one can testify firsthand on life after death, I have chosen the Holy Scriptures as my authority. They have withstood the test of time for millions of persons as they have faced death. Many heroically, many statistically. Many recounted in historical literature of our day. Many unnoticed in the days when no one cared to record such matters. But as for me and my house, we choose to rest our case with the Word of God. While making your decision, here are some verses that have meant so much to me.

• "In my Father's house are many rooms; if it were not so, would I have told you that I go to prepare a place for you?" (John 14:2, RSV).

• "And when I go and prepare a place for you, I will come again and will take you to myself, that where I am you may be also" (John 14:3, RSV).

• "For we know that if the earthly tent we live in is destroyed, we have a building from God, a house not made with hands, eternal in the heavens" (2 Cor. 5:1, RSV).

• "Lay up for yourselves treasures in heaven, where neither moth nor rust consumes and where thieves do not break in and steal" (Matt. 6:20, RSV).

• "But you have come to Mount Zion and to the city of the living God, the heavenly Jerusalem, and to innumerable angels in festal gathering" (Heb. 12:22, RSV).

• "But watch at all times, praying that you may have strength to escape all these things that will take place, and to stand before the Son of man" (Luke 21:36, RSV).

• "He will swallow up death for ever, and the Lord God will wipe away tears from all faces, and the reproach of his people he will take away from all the earth, for the Lord has spoken" (Isa. 25:8, RSV).

• "You foolish man! What you sow does not come to life unless it dies" (1 Cor. 15:36, RSV).

• "When the perishable puts on the imperishable, and the mortal puts on immortality, then shall come to pass the saying that is written:

'Death is swallowed up in victory' " (1 Cor. 15:54, RSV).

• "He will wipe away every tear from their eyes, and death shall be no more, neither shall there be mourning nor crying nor pain any more, for the former things have passed away" (Rev. 21:4, RSV).

• "And if children, then heirs, heirs of God and fellow heirs with Christ, provided we suffer with him in order that we may also be glorified with him" (Rom. 8:17, RSV).

• "And night shall be no more; they need no light of lamp or sun, for the Lord God will be their light, and they shall reign for ever and ever" (Rev. 22:5, RSV).

• "I consider that the sufferings of this present time are not worth comparing with the glory that is to be revealed to us" (Rom. 8:18, RSV).

• "For our light affliction, which is but for a moment, worketh for us a far more exceeding and eternal weight of glory" (2 Cor. 4:17).

• "We are of good courage, and we would rather be away from the body and at home with the Lord" (2 Cor. 5:8, RSV).

• "As life means Christ to me, so death means gain" (Phil. 1:21, Moffatt).

• "I am in a dilemma between the two. My strong desire is to depart and be with Christ, for that is far best" (v. 23, Moffatt).

• "But since to live means a longer stay on earth, that implies more labour for me—and not unsuccessful labour; and which I am to choose I cannot tell" (v. 22, Weymouth).

• "If we suffer, we shall also reign with him" (2 Tim. 2:12).

• "Henceforth there is laid up for me a crown of righteousness, which the Lord, the righteous judge, shall give me at that day: and not to me only, but to all them also that love his appearing" (2 Tim. 4:8).

• "And when the chief Shepherd shall appear, ye shall receive a crown of glory that fadeth not away" (1 Pet. 5:4).

The balance of this chapter is divided under three scriptural headings:

"Through a glass, darkly" (see 1 Cor. 13:12).

"O death, where is thy sting?" (see 1 Cor. 15:55).

"O grave, where is thy victory?" (see 1 Cor. 15:55).

Through a Glass, Darkly

The apostle Paul used this phrase as translated into modern English. However, there was no glass in the Middle East in Paul's day. The original word *glass* could be better translated "ancient mirror." Those mirrors did give a dark and cloudy image as well as a distorted one, similar to the ones in the side shows at the circus. It vividly portrays my feelings for taking a look at death. The view is incomplete and subject to your review. But it is one view—not arrived at easily.

Seeing through the glass darkly gives an image of the unknown. This is keenly felt by those of us who have perplexing health problems. And that usually means some degree of fear. We see death darkly. We see the future darkly. And although we hear about the brightness of heaven, we still have a blurred image of eternity. But for the Christian outlook, eternity is positive. For the non-Christian, it is questionable at best and spells disaster according to the teachings of Jesus. But let's take a hard look at death, even "through a glass, darkly."

When we leave this world, it leaves a lot to be desired. As you look at the international news on television tonight, is the world a pleasant place to be? Scan your local newspaper, and you will find the problems of the world are not all overseas, up North, or down South. When we leave this world, what have we left?

An obvious answer is loved ones. True, but will they not be expected to follow us to live with the Lord? (If not, we have a greater urgency pressed upon us to witness to them!) Do you actually think when our time comes to leave this world that we will have regrets? (If so, we'd better put this book down and attend to those matters of unfinished busines!)

At Niagara Falls hospital I had a good opportunity to take inventory on the balance sheet of eternity. Objectives were measured and evaluated. I had experienced and accomplished far more than I ever dreamed about: a wife and mother of a loving family, recently a grandmother, a bountiful circle of friends, a witnessing ministry, travel enough to broaden my perspective. And who would have imagined that I would author a published manuscript!

Oh, I have some fears of death: the fear that my illness will turn into bedfastness. To be waited upon and have no hope for any resemblance of a normal life, then the fear that Bob and the girls might die by accident before my passing. These thoughts surface when my emotional strength is low, and my spirit has not been recently nourished at the wellspring of faith. But with the regularity of the sun's rising in the east, I recall that God has taken care of me these many years. And he will continue to do so . . . Sonrise after Sonrise.

One of the sureties of death is that God will care for his own and raise them from the dead to new life. Reliably, 100 percent of the time. But for his own reasons, he does not heal his own 100 percent of the time during their stay on earth. Yes, "we see through a glass, darkly; but then face to face."

O Death, Where Is Thy Sting?

At least for twenty-plus years I have been looking over the grave and wondering what death would be like. That is not morbidity; it is reality. MS patients do not die directly of the disease. Rather, indirectly, like a urological failure owing to weakened muscles of the kidney or bladder or any vital organ whose muscles will not function properly. Then, too, anyone of us can die tomorrow from an accident.

If my sufferings have been overplayed, I apologize to you. It has not been my nature to exaggerate in any form, particularly when evaluating my characteristics and condition. But let me assure you that I would exchange the sufferings of this world in a minute for the joys of eternity. Hardly worthy of comparison! Do the lame want to walk? Do the depressed want peace? Do the weary want rest? Do the provoked want reconciliation? And on and on.

What do I have to give up? *Fame?* Hardly. You did not select this book from the shelf of the book store because my name is a household word. *Fortune?* Obviously not. (Bob is laughing.) There'll be no gathering of the clan to listen expectantly to the reading of my last will and testament. A legacy of Christian character I hope to leave but only a meager financial deposit. *Family?* Only temporarily. They will follow in the train of believers according to the Scriptures printed above.

How will I handle the death of Bob or the girls or even our sweet granddaughter if they precede me? Not as easily as my own. Life can go on even without them. They would be happier, and I would be even more dependent upon God's resources than I am today.

A Monologue

"Death, Who Do You Think You're Scaring?"
(Scene: The sky is dark outside today. The rain has brought accompanying muscle tightness. Things haven't gone too well recently. You could say the "blues" are just around the corner. I've just heard about the death of our "adopted" son and addressed these words to the death angel.)

"Hello, Death. Who do you think you're scaring? If you're so bold, why do you lurk behind the protection of the clouds. Come on out in the sun like a man. And why do you dress up in disguised clothing? Your nicely pressed white garments a la Prudential Life Insurance style doesn't make you any nicer. Your eternal black garb is just as farcical.

"You are somewhere between pristine white and ghoulish black. You are grey, for you are reality. Anything that is inevitable is real. But why can't I get my hands on you? And why can't I get my mind off of you? In spite of it all, you don't scare me a bit. Or do you? If not, why do I protest so much?

"No, you don't. I've reasoned you and your processes through my mental faculties. You're only a messenger of the news to be told. I can handle the message because it is good news. There is eternity waiting for me to live forever with God. So long, Death. Don't hang around here until you come with your first and only announcement of my earthly demise.

"Why are you still standing there, Death? And why am I weeping? Didn't I tell you that I had reasoned you out of my life until "death do us part?" Oh, it's my emotions you are playing on now, is it? Well, they have been played on before; but I'll admit, you do a better job than most. You ask, "What about loved ones left behind? And especially little Beth, your granddaughter?" You would bring her into this conversation. I have waited so long, and she is so lovable. But hold on, Death. I've gotten control of myself now, and I know that my Redeemer lives, so will I, so will Beth. So, along with you, Death. I'm not crying any hot tears for you.

"Now look at you, all dressed up in religious clothing, trying to fool me into thinking you represent the ritual of sadness. You think you're going to get a shot at my soul because your black stole has a golden cross embroidered on it? No, Death. You are out of your league when you want to joust with my soul. My mind and my emotions are flaky at times, but my soul rests secure.

"You see, Death, we mortals fall prey to your wizened chatter because you come from outside our world. Anyone ever call you "E.T.?" And we have difficulty thinking and feeling outside our own domain. But when you get into the world of the spirit, we are on common ground. Christ and I make a majority. I know I am his and his forever, whether limping along in this world or joyfully dancing in heaven.

"No, Death, I am not scared of you. Actually, when God gives you a message for me, I'll know my time has come to live with him. And you know what, Death? All you can do is escort me into his presence.

O Grave, Where Is Thy Victory?

How is it that the grave has double symbolisms with diametric directions? On one hand we see the grave as the end of it all. The curtain is rung down, and the comedy-tragedy is over. On the other hand, we see it as the beginning of a new life. The open tomb near Jerusalem is the epitome of hope. If you cannot comprehend this contradiction, think about it at your next Christian funeral.

We question some other branches of the Christian faith for their veneration of the flesh. Yet, consider our burial and funeral customs—what lengths (and expense) we go to in order to avoid the reality of the death of the body. It must seem odd to God and ridiculously funny to nonbelievers. Our bodies go from dust to dust, at least in symbolic form, regardless of our guarded words about death and our guarded steel vaults.

My body is fragile now and is expected to deteriorate with the years. It has been a semiprison for my soul. Why would I want to venerate it to be lost unto ultimate "dust"? Jesus taught so forcefully about the priority of spirit over the body that it seems our last and final act should bear witness to this truth. For this reason, Bob and I have given our bodies for medical research. It is our final declaration of the supremacy of the spirit.

Since there will be no grave at our funerals, what type of services are we planning? One of celebrating the successful completion of our pilgrimage on this earth, likewise the commencement of a new life in heaven with God and his children. A time without physical or emotional encumbrances. A time with little sorrow, grief, or disappointment. The music should be in a major key proclaiming the good news of salvation and eternity. The family and friends can have an opportunity to sing praises to God for his goodness and faithfulness. Eulogies can be reserved for those funerals where there is no good news to celebrate for the deceased.

Having no casket there will be no need for the grave, no symbol of men lowering my body into a darkened grave but rather the sure knowledge of God raising the spirit into the heavenly light. We don't want the family dutifully coming to the grave site in years to come and reading, "Here lies the body of Opha." To the contrary, we want any family or friend to be able to look to the heavens anytime and anywhere and declare: "There soars the spirit of Opha."

POSTSCRIPT (inserted at the last minute before going to press): Earlier this week my brother telephoned to give me word that mother had just died in the nursing home. It was expected, even hopefully anticipated. But we are never ready to give up our parents. How would I respond? My mind raced back to this chapter. Were my words only academic, or would I turn them into reality? To be honest I could not reliably predict until this week had passed.

It was a day to get the girls notified and ready to leave for the long day's drive to Lockwood, Missouri—the day of the funeral was typical in the ways of friends coming by, bringing food, offering condolences, and the like. But the funeral was not mournful and depressing. There was good news to tell and a celebration to experience. The local friends were not ready for Bob's upbeat comments at the graveside. But they welcomed the change from the customary "black crepe" environment.

Yes, I believe more strongly in a positive attitude towards death since mother's passing. Yes, I have been face-to-face with the separation of a beloved one. And yes, Virginia, there is life after death. It's like graduation day: a time to recall the memories past, a time to dream about the better days to come.

15
A Word from the Spouse

Now is the time for any good spouse to come to the aid of his mate. Is there a "word" appropriate to the role of the spouse? Is there a ministry to, and from, the mate of a person handicapped with a long-term illness? I think so.

Naturally, much of my feeling and experiences have been interwoven in Opha's previous chapters. Yet there are some matters that need to be surfaced from my viewpoint. And some hints to other spouses that spring from the same rootage.

Suffering is often vicarious. Pain and frustration endured by a loved one becomes internalized in the spouse. Waiting and watching, being unable to do little or nothing, develops its own pain. It's suffering in silence at best. How do you handle such emotions that are so intangible? *Very patiently. Very carefully. Very thankfully.*

Patiently because long-term, progressively deteriorating illness requires patience. More than I thought I could ever engender. There is the temptation to do things for her because I can do it better and faster. To take advantage of her handicapped situation when our disagreements become so heated I say things I want to retract. To go my own way and let her go hers. To ignore the common problems we face and think they will go away.

In these and similar situations . . . to lose my patience, to lose my temper, would be the beginning of losing the united effort that has made us more than conquerors over the fear that one day MS could drag us both down. Sometimes such negative emotions do fight their way to the surface, and when not curbed we suffer those pains that come from released words and feelings that should have been resolved prior to the crisis.

Like any other couple, these temptations can best be handled by sitting down and taking time to discuss them. However, when nerve endings are frazzled, somehow that is not considered a viable option. Genuine one-on-one open communication is the best therapy to bring about reconciliation. Why, then, is it so hard to practice it when you are upset? You tell me. Sometimes the best I can manage is to agree to discuss it later and walk away from the scene. Maybe our security is in the fact that we have promised to resolve our differences before going to bed.

Carefully because we are handling emotions that can so easily become bruised and fractured. And that damage is bad enough. But so often it is compounded with physiologically regression to the handicapped. The loss of temper becomes doubly costly. And it has never been worth the cost. There are some who counsel us to let our feelings be expressed out to the nerve endings. Generally, that seems good advice for my own emotional health. But what does it do to your mate who struggles against great odds to preserve her physical and emotional equilibrium? Hardly fair, is it? Like the giant abusing the little lad who doesn't even have five smooth stones.

And *thankfully* for several reasons. Because your good health can produce a strong arm against a fierce wind. Because you have the capacity to demonstrate your love in an arena for the whole world to take note of two lovers bound together by the bonds of common struggle. And because you can follow in the train of Christ who taught us to minister to those in need of healing graces. What a privilege to give a cup of cold water to your beloved day after day after day!

The Servant as Leader

Several months ago, an essay by the above title came across my desk. Written by Robert Greenleaf, it sets into perspective the teachings of Jesus relative to being a servant. He specifically makes the point that he did not mean, "The Leader as Servant." Like Jesus, he meant to place the primary emphasis on servanthood, not leadership. Many Christian leadership seminars miss this distinction and miss the basis of servanthood.

The stack pole illustration of the essay relates to a group of city folks who were taking a week's trip into the wilderness. They soon found that the hired cook was a true servant. There was nothing he would not try to do to convenience his guests. The days were filled with pleasure, and the trip went very well until one day when word came for the cook to go back to the ranch. Another cook came as a replacement, but the trip deteriorated from that point on. The campers took note and wondered why. When they returned to the ranch they learned the answer. The first cook was the owner of the ranch and the director of the camping trips. You see, he was the real "leader" of the camping group because he was a servant first.

Because of Opha's servant attitude, she is a real leader. Among friends of society, culture, business, religion; you name it, she stands tall. Given enough time for observation, comments such as these invariably arise: "Your wife is some kind of a lady." "She is the most courageous person I know." "It must be wonderful to live with a person like her." "Doesn't she ever give up?"

Such admiration basically comes from her obvious desire to serve others in spite of adversity. Opha is not an aggressive conversationalist. From her early days as a junior superintendent in Sunday School, she adopted the admonition of James, the half brother of Jesus: "Be ye doers of the word, and not hearers only" (Jas. 1:22).

Where does she exert her leadership? Primarily, in the two institutions she loves the most: her home and her church. In our case these two places have a deep penetration into the lives of many resourceful people. Perhaps it is not easy for you to understand her spiritual influence, unless you know her.

Take a look at our home. The house is not pretentious. Our entertaining is done in the den rather than a dining room. It is not what is in it but what comes out of it. Two loving and caring daughters. Nine "adopted" students. Literally dozens of friends who come to visit, to counsel, or to plan on some church or civic related project. These people are not quite the same after observing Opha as queen of the home and servant to the guests. She has the capacity of being both Mary and Martha in spite of her turtle pace. Guests leave with an appreciation of her homemaking arts. But they also leave with astonishment that she can be a loving servant in the tradition of Jesus. And in scorn of consequences. Countless friends have later recounted that they pledged to adjust their life-style because of her example and leadership.

And how could a back-pew worshiper be a prime leader of such a large and diverse congregation? Several words regularly come to the top: warm, smiling, determined, fearless, faithful, helpful, appreciative, caring, spiritual, dependable, selfless, humble, inspirational, and most of all: a Christlike person. Do you wonder why she is held in such esteem by so many fellow church members? The servant as leader?

In spite of such adulation, the years and years of increasing illness sometimes bore into her psyche. And drops of despair flowed to the surface. At such times she would ask, somewhat rhetorically, "Why don't I have the strength I need to do all the things I need to do? If God would only heal my body, I could serve him so much more effectively!" Even though she probably is not expecting an answer, I always give her the same response: "Opha, there must be tens of millions of healthy Christian ladies in the world. They serve the Lord as best they know. And the world looks on and says, 'There is a good lady.' But how many women are there in the world who let their light shine out of the clouds that encircle an MS patient of twenty years?"

How the Spouse Can Be of Help

Obviously, this is a personal matter. Help is directly related to needs. But there are some general concepts that seem to be common to those who must struggle with long-term illness. So here are some suggestions that have stood the test of time.

Priorities—In order to avoid the need for decision making time after time, decide to apply the principle of first things first. It may mean some adjustment to former life goals and priorities. But I had to recognize that a radical change had entered our married life-style, and some mid-course corrections were necessary.

1. Opha's needs were to take priority over my vocational pur-

suits and career objectives. This is a tough decision for most achievement-oriented persons. Especially, for the person in a religious vocation. This complication is the fine line between first commitments to Christ as compared to the commitments to the institutions of the Kingdom. I had these confused the first few years of her illness, and it led to a confused priority system. Finally, I realized that the primacy of my relationship to Christ did not mean that I was married to the church. This allowed me to function better as a husband and as a leader in the religious community.

2. Our daughters needed to know that I loved Christ more than my wife and loved my wife more than I loved them. The first affirmation is more than theological. It is actually supportive to the children. They understood that, because my highest commitment was to Christ, it meant they could depend on my actions towards them to be Christian. Likewise, Opha took courage that my priority to her, Christ, and the girls included the most important personages in her life.

3. Quality time together takes precedence over economic goals. Assuming that income provides a maintenance level of living, couples then must decide what is really important to gain life fulfillment. We feel that how we use our time is more important than ascending economic goals. In an earlier chapter Opha recounted how she faced me up to that decision with the skill of a surgeon's knife.

4. Attitudes are more important than actions. (These are complex and weighty matters, aren't they?) But it boils down to actions done out of poor motivations may be worse than no action at all. Handicapped persons depend so heavily on people's attitudes toward them. Sometimes, Opha must remind me that what I say is not as negative as the tone in which I say it. 'Nuff said.

5. I want to serve Opha because it is my privilege, not my duty. This is axiomatic to the heart of a servant. It is vital to the soul of the handicapped being served. Duty does not a marriage make. If serving is blessed, then how fortunate we are to be able to serve

the person we love the most. And in my case it is made so easy for she first served me. It is not hard to give her therapy each morning because she has just finished giving me a massage as I ease out of slumber into the dawn of a new day.

6. Ladies will be ladies. The feminine mystique is mysterious indeed to the male mind-set. But one of my priorities is to give her wide berth in exercising these feminine rituals. Weekly trip to the beauty parlor. Spending inordinate amounts of time getting dressed to go out. (Discounting that it naturally takes her longer. It is the "longer than that" which requires priority.) The need to go "shopping" when her closets are already full. The desire to have the house spic-and-span when no one is coming to visit. If years of experience had not already taught me about "the fairer sex," I was reminded of it while making a deacon's visit a few years ago. The lady inquired about Opha, and I shared the humor of my making peace with ladies "making up their faces." She brought me into feminine reality when she prophesied, "Bob, when a lady doesn't care how she looks, she is all washed up."

Specifics—So much for priorities. What about some specifics? Any spouse can give tremendous support, emotionally and physically, by choosing any of the following actions. If they appear trite to you, put yourself into the shoes of your spouse. Consider the condition, the length of illness or handicap, and the prognosis for improvement. It usually gives a different perspective on how to be helpful. I may be letting out more spousal secrets than spousal friends find comfortable. Hope they don't kick me out of the "Spouses' Union" for heresy. But remember, I make no claim for universal practicing of what I preach.

1. Keep your wedding vows in mind daily and renew them annually. The love message is distinct and exciting when kept alive.

2. Remember your Christian responsibility relates to your family as well as to the unsaved multitudes of the world.

3. Consider the need to redouble your parenting role of your children to pick up any slack caused by your spouse's physical impairment.

4. Alert family and friends of any major change in the condition of your mate. Objectivity and gentle candidness are necessary for all concerned. It's no time to play games.

5. Keep in touch with the medical profession and health aids. What a shame it would be if I knew the state of the art in model railroading but did not have time to read current information on MS medical research.

6. Try to keep your overachieving as subtle as possible. Let someone else note how much work you accomplish. To continually display this in front of your mate may become demoralizing to someone who already feels they accomplish so little.

7. Consider overprotection as a possible deterrent to your mate's growth. Every normal person retains the old childhood cliché, "I'd rather do it myself." Overprotection may inadvertently bring about a sense of insecurity.

8. Research in advance of any foreseeable barriers when your spouse goes outside the home environment. Awareness of such awkward situations usually gives opportunity to plan ways to avoid or minimize them.

9. Allow your spouse ways to accommodate you physically as well as emotionally. The blessing you receive will only be outweighed by the joy they receive in being able to accomplish it.

10. Take your mate into your confidence in matters relating to your vocational pursuits, long-range plans as well as day-to-day information. It took me a long time to realize that Opha wanted to be able to struggle with me on job-related problems. Formerly, I tried to shield her from them, and this only heightened her alienation from the world outside the home.

11. Remember the common courtesies that you extend to others in general should be extended to your spouse in particular. Opha still likes for me to seat her at the table, at home, or in public—as unpretentious as possible but as regular as taxes.

12. Allow spouses to be the center of attention when possible. In Opha's case, that is almost any time she is with friends. I refer to it as "The queen is holding court." More often than not we will be at a public function, and people will swarm about her leaving

me to love it from the sidelines. You cannot buy that kind of therapy. Encourage it.

13. Avoid using your spouse's handicap for your excuses. It is so easy to let people think you cannot attend or perform because your mate cannot do so. It really is demeaning to infer that your spouse is a burden to you when the fact is you are only flaking out yourself.

14. Plan some fun surprises. They are a lift to the spirit. You are aware of those most enjoyed. Make it happen.

How Family and Friends Can Help

Many of the hints listed above for the spouse can be adjusted and applied to family and friends. Here are a few additional ones for your consideration.

1. Accept people as real persons, recognizing that everyone is handicapped in some way. If you have not recognized your own, look for it. The search will do you good, and in turn you will be able to relate better to others.

2. Avoid making the handicapped person the center of attention or topic of conversation. If they are noteworthy in other ways, capitalize on those ways but not on their handicaps.

3. Exercise patience if the person is slow to function. They may be trying harder than you can imagine, but somewhere their system is malfunctioning.

4. Invite the person to be a participating member of your group. The tennis tournament might seem out of the question, but what about being the linesman or scorer?

5. Use simple words of encouragement but avoid flattery. It is an insult to their intelligence and degrading to their social growth.

6. Remember to encourage their families and friends: the first line of defense. These folks may be the unsung heros of the long fight of coping, and they need affirmation to keep on keeping on.

7. Be specific about the way you volunteer to help. It is not enough to casually comment, "Let me know if I can be of help." You may be sincere and willing to do anything to help. But you may not come across as genuinely eager to meet a need. Can you

imagine the good Samaritan looking down at the wounded traveler and saying, "Give me a call if I can help you"?

Why not take time to find out what is needed or would be
appreciated. Then volunteer by saying, "If you need someone to
_____, I'd be glad to do it one day this week."

8. Remember the person and family in your prayers. Take it
from us, there is no gift like regular prayer support. And don't feel
that it is immodest to tell the people that you are praying for them.
It provides a double blessing: know God hears and answers
prayers in addition to know people care enough to pray.

Questions Still in Transition

We have tried to be as objective as possible in sharing our
pilgrimage through these pages. But we're not fooling anyone,
including ourselves, that we have succeeded. In collecting material, making notes, writing the drafts, and finally editing the copy
—we blue-penciled out material in each stage that seemed extrane-
ous or in any way fictitious. Even so, subjectivity moves into a
manuscript like fog into the low country.

If it seems like we have it all wrapped up in a neat package, we
blew it. Our bodies tire more easily. Our nerves have more frazzles
than before. The only growth that approaches consistency is our
spiritual understanding of the realities of living and dying.

Yes, we still have unanswered questions. Some have been settled
once and for all. Some have been settled a hundred times and
unsettled a hundred times. Some are still in transition. Perhaps
they are worth surfacing for your consideration. If you have some
input to an eventual answer, why not write us. Hopefully, we are
still seeking. As for now, here are those questions:

1. Why has God allowed Opha to suffer so much and so long
in order to teach me some spiritual truths?

2. Why do some Christians exposit our catechism as it relates
to the eternal but live their lives as they relate to the here and now?

3. Why are there so many Job's friends in the Christian community?

4. Why do we preach the supremacy of the Spirit and practice the supremacy of the flesh?

5. Why do we think we can predestine God's will and actions by our personal or corporate prayers?

6. What makes me think Opha could not get along without me if I were to precede her in death? God has watched over her all these years. Is it not the supreme ego trip for me to think he must have me on the local scene to do his good works in her life?

One Final Word

How do you conclude such a story? By recycling? By just stopping? By making another appeal? Maybe it can best be summarized by quoting a famous author. We have chosen not to make the book a series of references of other writings. It is the account of one person's pilgrimage and responses.

So, how should it be concluded? In leafing through some notes and books, I came upon a handwritten note in the margin of Harold S. Kushner's classic, *When Bad Things Happen to Good People.* At the end of the chapter entitled "Why Do the Righteous Suffer?" I found these notes:

All things work together for good for those who love the Lord and are called according to His purpose.

Who?   —the believer
What?   —good things
When?   —now and forever
Where?   —here and eternity
Why?   —because God is: sovereign
                              love
                              just
                              full of grace.

Amen